assemble *v.t. & i.* the art of producing delicious food
with very little effort.

For Ted, Sean and Rose and good times together around the table.

Published in 2006 by
Grub Street
4 Rainham Close
London
SW11 6SS
Email: food@grubstreet.co.uk
Web: www.grubstreet.co.uk

Food Styling Annabel Langbein
Tablesettings and props Sarah Lods
Design Karryn Muschamp
Copy Editor Sally Butters
Typesetting and Production Natalie Keys for ICIP

A CIP catalogue for this book is available from the British Library

ISBN 1 904943 65 9

Printed and bound in India

Fresh oysters served with Thai sweet chilli dressing (previous page)

assemble
sensational food MADE SIMPLE

annabel langbein
photography nick tresidder

grub street | london

contents

Who cooks these days? Certainly we want to eat well but life is such a whirl that come the end of the day it seems we seldom have the time, let alone the energy, to even think about cooking. And it can be so fraught. When things go wrong it savages our confidence. So cooking has to be easy and you need to feel successful.

One of the main themes of this book involves taking a simple ingredient or cooking method and expanding it into different flavour profiles and ethnic styles. For instance, you can take lamb shanks and create a rich stew with Moroccan flavours, give it a French take with white beans and sausage, or bring in spicy Chinese flavours of ginger and star anise. The method is the same throughout. Very simple and very satisfying.

A good recipe should be like an easily read road map. If you follow the directions you arrive at your desired destination unstressed and in control. As you get to know the route you may find some nifty shortcuts. Confidence is the most important element you can bring to cooking and the more you cook, the easier it is. Cooking is not an exact science – things can go wrong. But don't worry or lose confidence. Most failures can be transformed.

Whether you are someone with a busy life who wants to be able to enjoy some home-prepared food without hassle or you are new to the kitchen, I hope that with this book in hand you will feel confident to start cooking and enjoy the process and the results.

Cooking is a celebration – of nature, friendship and family. Don't give yourself a hard time over any of your kitchen efforts. Know that people are grateful to be cooked for, no matter how simple your offerings. And just remember – they could all be eating takeout.

Enjoy.

Annabel

what it takes

Preparing food needn't be a chore. A few simple principles create a framework in which you can operate easily in the kitchen.

know that you don't have to be a great cook to produce great food

By shopping carefully for quality fresh produce and keeping a well-stocked pantry of flavours to draw on, you can put together with very little effort or skill vibrant-tasting food that you and the people you are feeding will enjoy and appreciate.

eat fresh

Base your meals around seasonal ingredients purchased from suppliers you trust. The better the ingredients the less work for you in the kitchen. Buy organic foods where possible and seek out artisan suppliers and organic growers with a commitment to sustainable farming practices.

utilise 'convenience' if it delivers

The increasing availability of prepared convenience foods offers some great short-cuts for the cook. Provided they are free of preservatives and artificial colours and flavours, quality prepared pasta sauces, fresh pestos and dressings, soups, flavour pastes and pastry are all value-adding ingredients I try to keep on hand as they are so useful. My philosophy is that if it is well made, delivers on flavour and texture and is versatile, use it. What you don't want is something you open once and then waste through not knowing other ways to use it. Add your own signature to commercial soups or sauces with a garnish or by adding extra ingredients to round out the taste or texture.

taste

Hey, this is what it's all about really – taste and, of course, texture. You have to taste food as you cook and, if you like, change ingredients or flavourings to suit your own palate. Building a memory wheel of flavours and textures helps immensely when you want to improvise or make judgements about combinations of foods and flavours.

be flexible

Apart from baking, which follows rigid laws of chemistry, most of the food we eat offers scope for interpretation and improvisation. If you don't have an ingredient that is listed, consider what might work as a substitute. Lots of the recipes in this book are based around a cooking style or method that can be applied to a wide range of ingredients.

seasoning

Probably the most important skill to learn in the kitchen is how to season food. Salt and pepper are the cook's greatest allies, and food cooked without them will always taste bland and flat. I have included quantities of salt for newcomer cooks so they can get used to knowing how much to use. If a recipe calls for lightly salted water (to boil vegetables, for example) use 1 tsp salt in a medium pot of water. Pasta requires more salt, about 1 tbsp per 1.5 litres (6 cups). For everyday cooking use regular table salt and save the expensive, boutique type such as Maldon and fleur de sel for table garnish or where the texture and subtle flavour can be enjoyed in a salad or as a bread topping.

set up a good pantry

This does not mean filling the shelves with ingredients that will languish unused for years. Rather it is ensuring that you have on hand the sort of things you like to eat. Starches such as pasta, rice and potatoes, flavourings, spices and condiments (see pantry essentials, pages 12-15) transform simple ingredients into something very interesting with little effort.

invest in a few good kitchen tools

You don't need much in the way of equipment to produce good food. To make everything in this book you will need a couple of really good sharp knives, a good chopping board (one side for sweet, one side for savoury), 3-4 good-quality pots, a couple of frypans that

won't pit or burn, a large cast iron casserole, a 3-litre baking dish, a roasting pan, a shallow baking tray, a set of mixing bowls, measuring spoons and cups, 2 Pyrex jugs, tools to handle food as it is cooking (tongs, spatulas, fish slices, etc), a lemon juicer, wooden spoon, whisk and hand beater. I consider a food processor or hand-held blender a 'must-have' appliance as it allows the production of a far greater range of food. You could also use a hand-held blender to blitz foods.

don't be too ambitious

When you first start out in the kitchen keep it simple. When you try a new dish and enjoy it, keep making it until you understand the process before starting to explore different flavour treatments using the same recipe base. It's a great way to build confidence as well as your own palate.

create some dining rituals

Regardless of the occasion or how simple the food being served, set the table with cutlery, napkins and water glasses, and light candles for evening dining. Invest in simple sets of crockery, cutlery and glasses so the table is not a mish-mash of styles. Food tends to look its best on plain white or cream plates. Take the time to enjoy the food and good conversation.

feel confident to cook for others

Lets face it, we all like being cooked for. The mere fact that you are bringing people together around the table to share a meal rather than eating takeout in front of the telly creates a sense of nourishment.

enjoy good wine

Most food tastes much nicer with a glass of something.

pantry
essentials

If you want to construct food without having to think ahead, you need a well-organized and well-stocked pantry. This does not mean buying a whole lot of ingredients that never get used, but rather thinking about the kind of food you like to eat and what you need to create interesting and appetizing tastes.

Anchovies Preserved anchovies should be firm and meaty and a deep, dark reddish-brown in colour. Ortiz is a good brand.
Storage Once opened, store anchovies in the fridge. If they are packed in salt, rinse and soak in several changes of water or milk before using.
Goes well with Caesar and other salads, pizza and pie toppings, rosemary, garlic, lemon, cream, pork, lamb, veal. For a good Caesar dressing see page 132.

Artichokes Preserved artichokes are a store cupboard mainstay. They are sold either in brine or flavoured oil.
Storage Once opened, refrigerate and use within a few days.
Goes well with pasta sauces, dips, oven bakes, sliced into a green salad with parmesan cheese. For a great dip see page 24.
Beans Canned beans – butter beans, cannellini, kidney, etc – offer lots of

scope to the cook. Drain and rinse before using. To eliminate any canned flavour, heat the beans in the microwave in a little olive oil with lemon zest and herbs.
Storage Once opened use within a couple of days.
Goes well with soups, stews, lamb, beef, chicken and pork.
Capers Best-quality capers are salted and require rinsing in several changes of water.
Storage Salted capers will keep for ages in the cupboard. Capers bottled in brine should be stored in the fridge once opened.
Goes well with seafood, chicken, parsley, sun-dried tomatoes, lemons, onions.
Chickpeas Drain and rinse before using.
Storage Once opened, keep in the fridge and use within a couple of days.
Goes well with salads, curries, soups, stews.
Chillies Useful in a range of forms from fresh chillies through to chilli pastes and sauces. Heat varies

tremendously. Habanero, aka Scotch bonnets, are one of the hottest, while Anaheim chillies are relatively mild. As a rough guide ½ tsp chilli flakes equal the heat of 1 small red bird's eye chilli.
Storage Keep a stash of fresh chillies in the freezer for use any time. Dried chillies, chilli flakes and sweet chilli sauce can be kept in the pantry.
Goes well with most ingredients, a little bringing them to life. For a great chilli dressing see page 128.
Chocolate (see page 208)
Storage Store in a cool pantry for several months.
Goes well with nuts, strawberries, baked goods. To melt 100g chocolate, place pieces in a microwave bowl and cook on high for 1 minute, stir and cook in 20-second bursts until it is sufficiently warmed to melt through when stirred. Do not over-heat or it may burn or clump together and be unworkable.
Coconut Cream (see page 144)

Goes well with curries and curry spices, fish, chicken, beef, pork, ginger, garlic, limes, chilli, vanilla, sugar. For a great red curry sauce base see page 144.

Curry paste Thai green and red curry pastes are available in a range of brands. They vary a lot in hotness so use less to start with and add more to taste until you get the heat you want. Write the amount used or heat quotient on the container for future reference.
Storage Once opened, store pastes in the fridge – they keep for ages.
Goes well with any dish where you want a spicy tone. Add to marinades and rubs, sauces and dressings.

Dashi Japanese soup stocks are collectively known as dashi. The most common dashi are made with kelp (kombu) or katsuo-bushi (dried bonito flakes). Commercial instant dashi is a powder made from dried bonito flakes. It makes a good stock base, especially for miso and sea-

food soups. Use 1½ tsp dashi for every 4 cups boiling water.
Storage Store powder in a cool dry place. It doesn't go off.

Fish sauce This pungent liquid confers a real depth of flavour. It is very salty so take care with additional seasoning. The smell disappears on cooking or mixing with other ingredients.
Storage Store in the pantry – it will keep indefinitely.
Goes well with any Asian flavourings, sauces, dressings and marinades. Using 1-2 tbsp in a curry or sauce gives it a real lift. For a low-fat dressing mix 2 tbsp fish sauce, 2 tbsp fresh lime juice, 1 tsp sesame oil and season with pepper.

Garlic Buy regularly, selecting fat, dense heads. To remove skins from garlic cloves bash them with the flat side of a heavy knife or cover with very hot water and leave for a few minutes then slip off skins. When cooking do not allow to become brown or it will be bitter.

Storage Store in a basket at room temperature.
Goes well with everything savoury, in any kind of ethnic flavour. Roasted garlic is a useful flavour that keeps well in the fridge. See page 15 for instructions on roasting garlic.

Ginger Fresh ginger is indispensable. It imparts a clean, fresh flavour.
Storage Store in a basket at room temperature. New season's ginger has thin, delicate skin like a new potato, and is soft and extremely perishable. As ginger ages the skins hardens to a rich gold and the flesh becomes more fibrous. The skin should be peeled off with the blunt top side of a knife before ginger is sliced or grated.
Goes well with all Asian and Moroccan flavours, and in desserts. A teaspoon or more of grated fresh ginger adds a zing to dressings and sauces. See page 148 for a useful ginger flavour base.

Goat's cheese and feta Keep on hand in the fridge for simple snacks and fillings.
Storage Once opened, store in olive oil or a salty brine, where it will keep for weeks.
Goes well with olives, herbs, chicken, lemons. Stuff under the skin of chicken, toss into couscous or pasta with pesto and toasted nuts, spread on to crostini or bruschetta.

Herbs Fresh herbs have the ability to add real freshness to

your food. If there is one herb not to be without it is parsley, as the addition of just a table-spoon or two can link the flavours and provide a sense of coherence to a dish. A basil plant does well on a sunny windowsill for longer than just summer, and other fresh soft herbs such as dill, chervil, mint and coriander are always useful.
Storage Store fresh herbs in a sealed container or plastic bag in the fridge. Provided they are dry they will last for over a week. Soft herbs such as basil and parsley freeze best when puréed with a little oil. Woody herbs such as thyme, rosemary and bay leaf can be frozen on the branch.
Goes well with anything for a boost of fresh flavour. Use mint, coriander and basil in combination for Asian dishes and basil, oregano and rosemary if you want a Mediterranean taste.

Icing sugar A dusting of icing sugar is the great redeemer, covering up mistakes and flops and disguising burnt bits.
Storage Keeps in a dry container for months.
Goes well with any sweet dessert. Sprinkle over foods before grilling to make a caramel topping.

Kaffir lime leaves These fragrant leaves are a feature of Thai and South-East Asian cuisine. As a substitute use the zest of 1 lime.

Storage Store in the fridge for several days in a sealed bag or freeze. Sometimes also sold dried.

Goes well with any Asian dish, lemons and limes, chillies, ginger, all meats, rice and noodles.

Kombu Dried seaweed used to flavour miso soup and Japanese soup stocks.

Lemon grass This aromatic grass adds a subtle flavour to stir-fries, sauces and oven bakes. Peel off the tough outer stem to reveal the white core at the base. Grate finely, discarding any fibrous stems. Or use whole stems bashed with the back of a knife to release flavour.

Storage Store in the fridge or place the root end in water – it will start to grow. Lemon grass can also be frozen.

Lemons and limes Quite possibly the most important ingredients you can have on hand to flavour food. Use zest (the finely grated outer skin which is full of essential oils) of 1-2 lemons in marinades, sauces, dressings and soups. Take care not to remove the inner white pith which is bitter. Lemon and lime juice add a fresh, clean taste.

Storage Keep in the fruit bowl or chill for longer life.

Goes well with everything. If adding to a milk-based sauce be sure the sauce is thickened and stable before adding lemon juice (or any other acid), otherwise it will curdle.

Mustard Dijon, whole seed, hot English and the milder French spreading mustard are all useful.

Storage Keep in the fridge.

Goes well with all meats, salad dressings, sandwiches.

Miso This rich, salty paste made from fermented soybeans and sometimes a grain such as rice is the essence of Japanese cooking. It is rich in proteins and calcium and low in fat and calories. Different ingredients and the period of aging produce different types of miso that vary in flavour, texture, colour and aroma.

Storage Store in the refrigerator, where it will keep for several months. The white mould that sometimes forms on miso is harmless. It can be scraped off.

Goes well with gravies and sauces, in a dressing or marinade. A tablespoon of miso mixed into a cup of hot water produces a satisfying broth to which other ingredients such as noodles, ginger and vegetables can be added.

Noodles Asian noodles differ from pasta in that they usually contain salt. Cook in boiling water, cool under cold water and drain. They can be cooked ahead of time and rinsed to separate just before using. Dried noodles more than double in weight on cooking.

Storage Noodles will keep in a sealed container for months.

Goes well with use wherever you want a starch base.

Oils (see page 126)

Olives Both green (immature) and black (mature) are inedible until they are cured, due to a very bitter glucoside called oleuropin. Salting olives is the traditional and most popular curing method. Chemical cures can make olives taste very bland.

Storage Olives are usually sold in brine. Sometimes a whitish mould develops on top of the brine. This can be removed and the olives will still be good to eat.

Goes well with all Mediterranean flavours and all protein. Marinate olives with herbs and spices for additional flavour.

Onions, spring onions, shallots Always have at least one of these on hand to add to a sauce, dressing or salad.

Storage Store dry-skinned onions and shallots in a basket in the pantry and spring onions in the fridge.

Goes well with everything.

Oyster sauce Useful Asian sauce made from oyster extracts. It has a smoky, salty taste and flavour-enhancing qualities.

Storage Once opened, store in the fridge – it will keep for several months.

Goes well with all Asian flavours, as a sauce for pan-fried steak with a little honey, and as a marinade for beef and chicken.

Parmesan (see page 84)

Pesto (see page 18)

Prosciutto/parma ham Salt-cured, air-dried, raw Italian ham. Pressing during processing makes it firmer than other hams. Purchase paper-thin slices and serve fresh with bread or fruits such as melon or figs.

Storage It will keep in the fridge in greaseproof paper for several days.

Goes well with bread, figs, melon, peaches. Fry and serve with salad greens. See salad on page 119.

Rice paper (see page 33)

Roasted garlic Slice off the top of a whole bulb of garlic to expose cloves and place in a heatproof ramekin. Pour over about ½ cup olive oil and bake at 150°C for 35-45

minutes until tender. Allow to cool then squeeze garlic purée from husks. Mix with oil from cooking.

Storage Store in the fridge – it will keep for ages.

Goes well with pastas, dressing, sauces and stews. Roasting garlic in oil produces a mellow buttery paste, ideal for using as a flavouring.

Roasted peppers Wash red, yellow or green peppers and roast in a 220°C oven until they start to blister and brown, 15-20 minutes. Remove and place in a covered container or plastic bag until cool enough to handle. Remove skin, seeds and pith from peppers under cold running water. Slice peppers into strips and mix with a little olive oil.

Storage Refrigerate for up to 1 week or freeze.

Goes well with pasta sauces, salads, stews and oven bakes, frittata or pie fillings.

Semi-dried tomatoes Purchase these at a delicatessen or, if unavailable,

soak sun-dried tomatoes in water for 20 minutes to semi-soften then slice.

Storage These will keep in oil in the fridge for months.

Goes well with pasta dishes, salads, casseroles, pizza, pies, frittata.

Saffron The dried stigmas of the saffron propus (*Crocus sativus*) are the world's most expensive spice. Saffron quality is graded by colour. The thread-like stigmas should be a deep red, any white or light patches are inferior. Saffron requires hot liquid to release its colour. Do not add butter or oil without first infusing it.

Storage Kept in a dark dry place, it will last for years.

Goes well with seafood, sauces, potatoes, Moroccan flavours. Ten to twelve threads are enough to give flavour.

Sesame oil The nutty flavour of sesame oil is a great foil for Asian dishes. Toasted sesame oil is darker and more strongly flavoured than regular.

Storage Store in a cool place and check smell before using. Rancid oils are toxic and should be avoided.

Goes well with any Asian dishes. It has a low burn temperature so if heating, mix with another oil or add at the end of cooking.

Soy sauce A staple used in both China and Japan. Chinese varieties tend to be made of fermented soya

beans and come in two strengths – light and dark. Dark soy sauce is more commonly used in cooking as its flavour develops with heating. Japanese soy sauce or shoyu tends to include wheat which gives it a sweeter flavour. Tamari, which is darker and richer in flavour again, is traditionally the liquid that runs off miso as it matures.

Storage Store in the pantry – it keeps for ages.

Goes well with any Asian dish. Adds a salty flavour so check before you add salt.

Spices Buy small amounts from a supplier who turns them over quickly. Toasting and grinding before use releases essential oils in spices and develops better flavours.

Storage Store in sealed containers and replace often.

Goes well with anything.

Stock (see page 92)

Vanilla Use natural amber-coloured extract or whole beans. Avoid synthetic vanilla.

Storage Store vanilla pods in a sealed container.

Goes well with any dessert. Split whole vanilla beans lengthwise and heat in milk or other liquid, scraping in the seeds for extra flavour.

Vinegar Keep a range of different vinegars to add balance and an acid element.

Storage Stored in the pantry, it will keep indefinitely.

Goes well with sauces and dressings.

fridge essentials

Zingy pastes and dressings unify the elements of a dish and can elevate simple, everyday ingredients to something that tastes as if it has taken a lot of effort to prepare. Buy or make these flavour 'starting points' and have them on hand in the fridge.

salsa verde

30 g (about 2 handfuls) basil leaves

15 g mint (about 1 handful)

4 tbsp chopped chives

2 tbsp capers

2 cloves garlic, peeled

2 tsp Dijon mustard

4 tbsp lemon juice

250 ml olive oil

5 anchovy fillets

¼ small red onion, chopped

optional 1 hard-boiled egg yolk

PURÉE all ingredients together until smooth.

Makes 500 ml

Storage Keep in the fridge for up to a week or freeze.

basil pesto

60 g (about 4 handfuls) basil leaves

2 large cloves garlic, crushed

185 ml good-quality olive oil

4 tbsp grated parmesan

½ tsp salt & grinds black pepper

optional 4 tbsp pine nuts or walnuts, toasted

PURÉE all ingredients together in a food processor until smooth. Or pound with a mortar and pestle, adding oil once the mixture forms a fine paste.

Makes 375 ml

Storage Store in the fridge for up to 2 weeks or freeze in small containers.

tapenade

125 g stoned kalamata olives

1 clove garlic, crushed

4 anchovy fillets

1 tbsp capers

zest of ½ lemon

5 tbsp olive oil

PURÉE all ingredients together into a smoothish paste.
SERVE with crostini (page 24).

Makes 250 ml

Storage Tapenade will keep in the fridge for months.

pantry flavour bases

Flavoured oils and mayonnaises are useful taste bases that offer a delicious conduit for combining various salad ingredients. As an alternative to using fresh herbs, mix good-quality pesto with enough oil to create a spoonable consistency.

basil oil

60 g (about 4 handfuls) basil leaves
½ tsp salt
250 ml oil, eg grapeseed or olive oil or a mix of both

PLACE basil leaves in a bowl and pour over boiling water to wilt. Drain at once and refresh under cold water.

DRAIN thoroughly and purée with salt and oil until smooth. Strain off solids through a fine sieve if desired (I don't bother).

Makes 375 ml

Storage Keep in the fridge up to 4-5 days or freeze in ice block containers.

■ Mint Oil
Substitute mint for basil.

■ Rocket and Parsley Oil
In place of basil use a handful of rocket leaves – 6-8 quite large leaves – and 2 handfuls of Italian parsley, tough stems removed.

■ Lime Chilli Coriander Oil
In place of basil use 2-3 coriander plants, roots removed, 1 small red chilli, seeded, and the zest of 1 lime. Good for Asian dishes.

fresh lemony mayonnaise

4 tbsp lemon juice
3 fresh egg yolks
1 tsp salt
½ tsp fine pepper
zest of 1 lemon
250 ml flavourless oil, eg grapeseed, or 50/50 mix of olive oil and flavourless oil

PLACE all ingredients except oil in a food processor and blitz to combine. With motor running, slowly add oil in a thin stream until mixture thickens to a creamy sauce. (If it gets too thick, thin with a little hot water.)

Makes 300 ml

Storage Mayo will keep in the fridge for up to 2 weeks.

Use fresh lemony mayonnaise or a good-quality commerical mayo to make the following:

■ Chermoula Dressing
125 ml mayonnaise, 8 tbsp chopped coriander leaves, 2 cloves garlic, crushed, 1 tbsp lemon juice, ½ tsp smoked paprika or paprika, 1 tsp ground cumin and ¼ tsp cayenne pepper.
COMBINE all ingredients.
Makes 185 ml

■ Wasabi Lime Mayo
125 ml mayonnaise, 2-3 tsp wasabi paste, 2 tbsp lime juice
COMBINE all ingredients.
Makes 125 ml

■ Curry Mayonnaise
125 ml mayonnaise, 1 tbsp lime or lemon juice, 1 tsp good-quality curry powder, ½ tsp brown sugar
WHISK all ingredients together.
Makes 125 ml

snack

You don't have to start from scratch to make great nibbles and finger foods. Buy ready-made snacks (as long as they taste really good) and give them your own signature with a drizzle of the best olive oil, a grating of lemon zest or parmesan, or a sprinkle of paprika or fresh herbs. Using fresh produce provides a seasonal focus to the dishes you serve. Offer crisp cucumber wedges with a creamy smoked salmon dip, lightly cooked green beans and asparagus with a bowl of salsa verde or pesto, new season's radishes with flavoured butters, or cos lettuce leaves with a garlicky Caesar dressing.

Fresh, lightly cooked asparagus served with salsa verde and a glass of wine makes a casual snack

blitz together
cream cheese with...

Use cream cheese or mascarpone as a base for a range of excellent dips and spreads. Simply blitz all ingredients in a food processor until smooth. These dips will keep in the fridge in covered containers for up to a week, or can be frozen.

250g cream cheese
100g smoked salmon pieces
2 tbsp lemon juice
2 tbsp chopped fresh dill or fennel or Italian parsley
1 tbsp capers

smoked salmon and caper pâté
Serve this creamy pâté with rounds of fresh cucumber or enjoy it in sandwiches or on crispbread. It can also be rolled up in slices of smoked salmon or served with fresh asparagus and salad greens.
Makes 425 g

250g cream cheese
125 ml cream
4 anchovy fillets
1 tbsp capers
2 tsp chopped fresh tarragon or parsley
2 cloves garlic, crushed
zest of ½ lemon

creamy cheese and herb dip
This creamy, tangy dip is terrific on a platter piled with mixed roasted and fresh vegetables, breads and olives. It also makes a great filling for chicken breasts. Add more cream to turn it into a dipping sauce for green beans or asparagus, or heat until melted and serve over cooked steak, seafood or chicken.
Makes 425 g

200g feta, crumbled
125g cream cheese
3 tbsp olive oil
1 small red chilli or ½ tsp chilli flakes
½ tsp fennel seeds

feta chilli and fennel dip
Blending feta with cream cheese gives it a wonderfully unctuous texture that's great for spreads and fillings. It's also good baked in red pepper halves or used with fresh spinach leaves as a stuffing for lamb.
Makes 375 g

QUICK CREAMY DIP IDEAS
Mix cream cheese or mascarpone with:

■ A spoonful of your favourite pesto, chutney or relish

■ Crushed ginger and garlic, fresh coriander and a little sweet chilli sauce

■ Pesto and grated parmesan

■ Dried onion soup powder and chopped fresh chives

■ Flaked smoked fish, lemon juice and dill or parsley

open a can

When you need a speedy snack for guests, make use of quality canned foods such as tuna, tomatoes, anchovies, artichokes and beans. Thinking of these ingredients as classy preserves rather than as canned foods makes them seem less processed.

400g can artichokes, drained
85 ml extra virgin olive oil
4 tbsp chopped coriander
8 kalamata olives, pitted and chopped
3 anchovy fillets
2 cloves garlic, crushed

tuscan artichoke spread

BLITZ everything together to a slightly chunky paste. SERVE as a dip for fresh vegetables or use as a bruschetta spread. Mix through cooked potatoes as a side dish to serve with steaks and barbecue meats, or toss through cooked pasta (see page 50).

Makes 500 g

Storage Spread will keep in the fridge for up to a week.

185g can tuna, drained
60 ml cream
1 gherkin, finely chopped
1 tsp capers, chopped
1 tsp thyme leaves
½ tsp grainy mustard
¼ tsp salt & grinds of pepper
zest of ½ lemon

niçoise tuna dip

BLITZ or purée all ingredients together until smooth. SERVE as a dip for fresh vegetables or use as a bruschetta spread. Mix through cooked potatoes as a side dish to serve with steaks and barbecue meats, or toss through cooked pasta (see page 50).

Makes 300g

Storage Dip will keep in the fridge for 2-3 days.

CRISPBREADS AND CROSTINI

Thinly slice a flat loaf, eg pide or focaccia, or for crostini slice a French stick. Spread on a baking tray and spray or brush with olive oil. Bake at 180°C until golden and crisp, 20 minutes. Cool and store in an airtight container. These will keep about a week and can be recrisped in a hot oven for 5 minutes.

grab a bag of beans

400g shelled and
peeled broad beans
50 g finely grated pecorino or
parmesan
4 tbsp extra virgin olive oil
20 mint leaves, finely chopped
4 anchovy fillets
2 garlic cloves, crushed
½ tsp salt & grinds of pepper

broad bean, mint and pecorino spread

PLACE everything in a food processor and blitz to a chunky purée, adding a little oil or water to thin as preferred. You can use thawed frozen broad beans (slip the skins off), or cook fresh beans for 3-4 minutes in lightly salted boiling water, drain and cool then slip the skins off. Spread on bruschetta (page 45).

Makes 500 g

Storage Spread will keep for 4-5 days in the fridge.

400-500g green beans
250 ml quality mayonnaise
2 tbsp miso
2 tbsp grated fresh ginger
1 clove garlic, crushed
2 tsp brown sugar
1 tsp sesame oil
1 tsp soy sauce

green beans with miso sauce

TRIM ends from beans. Boil in lightly salted water for 3 minutes. Refresh under cold water and drain.
COMBINE remaining ingredients to make miso sauce. Serve beans with miso sauce drizzled on top.
This sauce also makes a terrific dressing for asparagus, leafy salads, noodles, and seafood and chicken salads.

Makes 425 g

Storage Cook beans just before serving. Miso sauce will keep in the fridge for up to 1 week.

JAPANESE SOY BEANS

At last, an addictive snack that's actually good for you! You'll find soy beans in the freezer of Asian supermarkets – keep a stash in your own freezer. The beans have been blanched so they only need to be heated through before serving. Steam or microwave them until hot, about 2-3 minutes, pile into a serving bowl and sprinkle with flaky sea salt. To eat, pop beans out of their shells with your teeth and discard the shells. A 500g pack will serve 4-6 people as a snack.

dress up seafood

Classic combinations never go out of date. When you want something smart to serve to your in-laws or for a swanky drinks party, start here. Be sure the seafood comes with impeccable credentials.

125 ml quality mayonnaise
2 tbsp tomato ketchup
1 tsp worcestershire sauce
optional: ½ tsp diced chilli

300g prawn tails, cooked
½ iceberg lettuce, thinly sliced
½ cucumber peeled into thin strips with a potato peeler

classic prawn cocktail

COMBINE mayonnaise, ketchup, worcestershire sauce and chilli. Store sauce in the fridge until ready to serve. Serve with prawn tails, lettuce and cucumber.

Makes 185 ml sauce, serves 6
Storage Sauce will keep in the fridge for up to a week.

100g butter, softened
2 tsp wasabi paste
zest of ½ lemon
2 tsp lemon juice
pinch each salt and pepper

2 dozen fresh oysters
24 slices wholegrain bread cut into 4cm rounds
extra lemons and pepper

oysters with wasabi-buttered bread

MIX butter with wasabi, zest and juice and seasoning. Spread bread lightly with wasabi butter and top each round with an oyster. Squeeze over a little lemon juice and grind over black pepper.

Makes 2 dozen
Storage Wasabi butter will keep in the fridge for several weeks and is also terrific used to pan-fry lightly floured fish fillets.

quail eggs with herbs

12 quail eggs, 2-3 tbsp finely chopped soft herbs (eg chervil, parsley and chives), ½ tsp salt

BOIL quail eggs for 5 minutes (or hen eggs for 10 minutes), cool and shell. Mix herbs with salt. Roll eggs in herbs, slice in half with a very sharp knife and arrange cut side up on a platter.

Other coatings Coat eggs with celery salt or dukkah.

Serves 4

Storage Cooked, unpeeled eggs will keep in the fridge for 2-3 days. Once peeled they should be eaten within a couple of hours or they will dry out.

prosciutto breadsticks

20 fresh rocket leaves, 10 breadsticks, 10 thin slices prosciutto

HOLD 2 fresh rocket leaves along each breadstick and tightly wrap around a thin slice of prosciutto or parma ham.

Makes 10

Storage Make up to 2 hours ahead and chill.

■ **Smoked Salmon Breadsticks**

Spread cream cheese on to sticks before attaching leaves. Use very thin slices of smoked salmon instead of prosciutto.

salmon and cucumber rolls

4 cooked savoury crêpes (buy or make, page 39), 3 tbsp cream cheese (or a cream cheese dip, page 23), 8 slices smoked salmon, 8 batons cucumber or lightly cooked asparagus, cooled

SPREAD each crêpe with cream cheese. Cover each with 2 slices salmon and top with a baton of cucumber or asparagus. Roll up tightly, securing rolls with a dab of cream cheese. Slice each roll into 4 pieces. Allow 2-3 pieces per serve.

Serves 4-6

Storage Prepared rolls can be kept covered in the fridge for up to 12 hours.

radishes with butter

1 bunch freshest radishes, 50g plain butter or wasabi butter (page 28)

WASH and place on a platter with a small bowl of softened butter or wasabi butter.

Serves 4

Storage Radishes will stay fresh for 2-3 days stored in a sealed bag or container in the fridge.

wrap it up

These are nice to serve for a weekend brunch, a light lunch or a pre-movie snack. I tend to think of them as 'girls' food', maybe because they are so light and fresh. That said, I don't know of anyone, male or female, who doesn't go mad for them.

50g rice vermicelli
16-20 large cooked shrimps, chopped
1 carrot, peeled and grated
50g finely shredded crisp lettuce
30 g coriander or mint leaves or a mix of both
10 round rice papers

prawn salad rolls

POUR boiling water over vermicelli to cover and stand for 10 minutes to soften. Drain thoroughly and set aside.
COMBINE all remaining ingredients (except rice papers). Thoroughly wet a clean tea towel, squeeze out excess water and lay on a clean bench.
FILL a bowl with hot water. Dunk each rice paper into hot water, count to 2, remove at once, shake off excess water and lay on damp towel. After about a minute the rice papers will soften to a workable texture.
PLACE some vermicelli and ¼ cup filling across the top third of paper. Fold in the sides of the wrapper then roll up very tightly to enclose the filling. Accompany with peanut dipping sauce (page 36).
Makes 10 rolls, serves 4-5
Storage Rolls can be made, covered and chilled for up to 6 hours. Cover prepared rolls with a damp paper towel then wrap tightly in plastic wrap and chill.

HANDLING RICE PAPERS

These South-east Asian pastry wrappers need to be softened before use. Dip individual sheets quickly into hot water or brush both sides with hot water, and after a minute or two the sheets will be soft and workable. They can then be filled and served fresh or deep-fried.

Once you have the hang of rice paper wraps use them to make all kinds of quick salad rolls. Prawns, Chinese barbecue pork, cooked chicken or duck all work well as fillings, or simply make the rolls with salad vegetables and herbs.

33

roll a crispy parcel

I always bake these rather than fry them and the results are just as crisp and appealing. Don't think only Asian flavours here, as the crunchy wrappers will take well to any kind of filling you fancy. The rolls can be prepared ahead and chilled ready for baking.

AROMATIC FLAVOUR BASE
2 tbsp sweet chilli sauce
2 tbsp chopped coriander
1 tbsp fish sauce
1 tsp finely grated fresh ginger
1 tsp minced lemon grass
greens of 1 spring onion,
finely chopped
1 clove garlic, crushed

flavour base (see left)
300g lean pork mince
100 g finely shredded
Chinese cabbage or
regular cabbage
1 egg white
15 spring roll wrappers
oil to brown, about 4 tbsp

crispy pork rolls

MIX flavour base with mince, cabbage and egg white until evenly combined.

PLACE 2 tbsp mixture on each wrapper, fold in ends and roll up tightly like a fat cigar. Brush with oil and place on a baking tray lined with baking paper. Chill until ready to cook, up to 4 hours.

BAKE at 190°C until golden and crisp, about 20 minutes.

Serves 5-6

■ **Crispy Chicken Rolls**
Use 300g chicken mince instead of pork.
■ **Crispy Prawn Rolls**
Use 300g minced prawn meat instead of pork.

150g feta, crumbled
1 chopped roasted red
peppers
2 tbsp basil pesto
12-15 pitted olives
1 egg white

mediterranean vegetable rolls

COMBINE ingredients, fill wrappers and bake as for crispy pork rolls (above).

SERVE with chilli lime dipping sauce (page 36).

50g slice of fresh boneless
salmon
1 tbsp pesto

salmon rolls

PLACE a piece of salmon on each wrapper.

TOP with 1 tbsp pesto (or sweet chilli sauce or other flavouring of your choice). Roll up and bake as for crispy pork rolls (above).

do the salsa

Some of the best meals are the simplest – a succulent piece of grilled, barbecued or roasted meat or fish served with a green salad, potatoes or bread and a fresh sauce or salsa to provide a personal finishing touch.

4 tbsp sweet chilli sauce
2 tbsp fresh lime juice
1 tbsp fish sauce
2 tsp chopped coriander or mint
finely chopped greens of 1 spring onion

chilli lime dipping sauce

Mix all ingredients together and spoon into a serving bowl.
Makes 125 ml
Storage Sauce will keep in the fridge for 2-3 days.

diced flesh of 2 mangos, fresh or canned
2 tbsp sweet chilli sauce
2 tbsp fresh lime or lemon juice
2 tbsp chopped fresh coriander

fresh mango salsa

MASH or roughly purée mangos and combine with remaining ingredients.
Makes 500-750 ml
Storage Salsa will keep well up to 12 hours in the fridge.

3 tbsp sweet chilli sauce
4 tbsp peanut butter
2 tbsp chopped roasted peanuts
2 tbsp lime juice
1 tbsp fish sauce
1 spring onion, finely diced

peanut dipping sauce

MIX everything together until evenly combined.
Makes 425 ml
Storage Serve within a few hours before peanuts soften.

OTHER USEFUL SAUCES AND SALSAS

■ Avocado and tomato guacamole (page 122)

■ Green goddess dip (page 122)

■ Salsa verde (page 16)

■ Flavoured mayonnaises (page 18)

■ Tapenade (page 16)

■ Caesar dressing (page 132)

■ Pesto (page 16)

■ Fresh tomato salsa (page 43)

■ Miso sauce (page 26)

■ Soy sesame dressing (page 128)

fry a fritter

The versatility of this batter makes it a must-have in any cook's repertoire. Add any flavours you fancy and cook outdoors on the barbecue or inside in a pan.

175 g plain flour
3 tsp baking powder
3 eggs
250 ml chilled soda water
or cold water
½ tsp salt & grinds of pepper
fritter flavours of your choice
2-3 tbsp flavourless oil (eg grapeseed) for frying

fritter batter base

COMBINE flour, baking powder, eggs, soda water or water, salt and pepper in a mixing bowl, beating to make a smooth batter. Cover and store in the fridge until ready to cook – up to 4 hours ahead.
MIX in fritter flavours (see below/over for ideas).
HEAT a heavy frypan over medium heat and spray lightly with oil. Cook dessertspoonfuls of mixture, 2-3 at a time, turning to cook the other side as bubbles form in the mixture. Lightly re-oil pan between batches. Transfer cooked fritters to a rack.

1 recipe fritter batter base
(above)
30 g finely chopped mixed soft herbs, eg basil, parsley, chervil, mint
4 tbsp lemon juice
zest of 1 lemon
goat's cheese
watercress

lemon herb fritters with goat's cheese

PREPARE fritter batter base (above) and stir in all other ingredients except goat's cheese and watercress.
COOK as above.
TOP with goat's cheese and a sprig of watercress.
ACCOMPANY with a green salad or with a dipping sauce if serving as finger food.
Makes 24 medium or 60 small fritters
Storage Cooked fritters can be chilled for up to 12 hours and reheated in a hot oven for 5-6 minutes.

FRITTER TIPS

■ Add flavourings of your choice to the basic batter

■ Fritters can be made ahead and reheated in a hot oven for 5 minutes

■ They can also be cooked in tiny spoonfuls and served as finger food

■ Cut pan time by frying fritters until just browned on either side then transferring them to an oven dish and baking at 180°C until cooked through, about 5 minutes

SAVOURY PANCAKES

Add 185 ml milk and 2 tbsp melted butter to the fritter batter. Cook in large spoonfuls like fritters.

For the following recipes, prepare the fritter batter base on the previous page, stir in flavours and cook.

corn, mint and feta fritters

600-750g corn kernels
100g crumbled feta
3 tbsp chopped fresh mint

coconut fish fritters

200g raw fish or seafood, diced
8 tbsp desiccated coconut
zest and juice of ½ lime
green of 1 spring onion, finely chopped

chilli, courgette and smoked mussel fritters

125g chopped cooked mussels or other seafood
1 courgette, grated
4 tbsp chopped coriander
zest and juice of 1 lemon
1 red chilli, finely chopped or ½ tsp chilli flakes

sour cream and chive dipping sauce

125 ml sour cream
zest and juice of 1 lemon
2 tsp chopped chives
COMBINE ingredients and serve with fritters.
Makes 125 ml

dip a chip

Bring on the tequila shooters or whip up some cool mint mojitos and open a big bag of crisp corn chips. Make it a party with tasty tomato salsa, spicy bean dip and a creamy avocado and tomato guacamole (page 122).

black bean nachos

250-300g corn chips
100g grated mozzarella
400g can black beans, drained
250 ml tomato salsa
1 red chilli, finely chopped
4 tbsp chopped coriander
½ tsp salt & grinds of pepper
50-80g feta, crumbled

PILE corn chips in a heatproof bowl, cover with mozzarella and microwave until cheese melts, about 2 minutes.
COMBINE beans, salsa, chilli, coriander and seasoning. Spoon sauce over chips, sprinkle with feta and place under a hot grill until heated through, 2-3 minutes.
SERVE at once. Accompany with a bowl of chilli sour cream made by mixing 3 tbsp sweet chilli sauce with 250 g sour cream.
Serves 4 as a snack or 2 as a light meal

spicy bean dip

425g can red kidney beans
125g sour cream
125 ml tomato salsa
2 tbsp chopped coriander
2 tsp ground cumin
1 clove garlic, crushed
½ tsp salt & grinds of pepper

DRAIN kidney beans and mash roughly with remaining ingredients.
SERVE with corn chips or pita toasts.
Makes about 375 ml
Storage Keeps for several days in the fridge.

fresh tomato salsa

4 tomatoes, finely diced
1 small onion, finely diced
1 red chilli, finely chopped
2 cloves garlic, crushed
4 tbsp chopped coriander
2 tbsp lime juice
½ tsp each salt, ground pepper and sugar

COMBINE all ingredients and stand at least 30 minutes before serving to allow flavours to develop. Accompany with corn chips and tequila shooters.
Makes about 750 ml, enough for 6-8 servings
Storage Keep in the fridge and eat within 24 hours.

slice a rustic loaf

Start with a baker's loaf – something dense and substantial, a good sourdough or country loaf. Serve a platter of mixed bruschetta for a lazy lunch or let people assemble their own from a platter of toppings.

bruschetta bases

Cut a sourdough or country loaf into slices about 5mm thick. Brush with olive oil and grill or brown on a griddle. Bases are best made the day they are to be served. Serve each bruschetta with toppings of your choice.

toppings

tomato and mozzarella

Rub a cut tomato over prepared bruschetta, top with sliced fresh mozzarella, sliced tomato and a spoonful of basil oil or pesto.

rocket, feta and tapenade

Mix equal quantities of cream cheese and feta until smooth. Put 2 rocket leaves on each bruschetta base and top with cheese and a teaspoon of tapenade.

blue cheese, pear and prosciutto

Spread prepared bruschetta with blue cheese. Top with slices of fresh pear and a thin slice of prosciutto.

salmon, red pepper and capers

Spread prepared bruschetta with cream cheese. Top with slices of smoked salmon and roasted red pepper. Garnish each one with a few capers.

assemble
a platter

Arrange the following ingredients to create the platter of your choice.
Focus on quality and a good wine match. Each of these platters will
serve 6 people.

fontainbleu platter

150g salami
150-200g ripe goat's cheese
50g thinly shaved prosciutto
1 French stick
2 fresh apples
1 pkt crispbreads

vegetable lovers' platter

1 recipe broad bean, mint and pecorino spread (page 26)
1 recipe Tuscan artichoke spread (page 24)
300g asparagus, lightly cooked
2-3 roasted red peppers
2 French sticks

caesar's platter

125 ml Caesar dressing (page132)
300g fresh asparagus or beans, lightly cooked
12 prosciutto and rocket breadsticks (page 30)
10-15 long, crisp crostini

gorgonzola platter

250-300g ripe gorgonzola
2-3 ripe juicy pears
6-8 fresh dates or figs
1 French stick

hot light meals

Hot food appeals to our appetites with a sense of nourishment that cold food seldom achieves.

Aside from the 'open the can' or 'heat and eat' scenarios of commercially processed food, one assumes that hot food requires a greater level of involvement and therefore effort than any quick collations of salad ingredients or sandwiches. In fact the effort required to produce an appetising hot dish is minimal, provided you choose a simple starting point. Even better, delivering hot, home-cooked dishes to the table will guarantee your reputation as a cook. Whether you are boiling a pot for some pasta to toss with a quick sauce or heating a pan for an omelette, the results are extremely satisfying.

mix and serve ...
flavours for pasta

Texture is paramount when it comes to pasta. Good-quality dried pasta, either organic or artisan produced, will hold its texture and, if it has been produced by bronze extrusion, will have tiny ridges on the outer surface that allow the sauce to cling rather than slip off.

200g quality dried pasta
3 tbsp Tuscan artichoke spread (page 24) or use commercial artichoke paste
2-3 slices prosciutto, fried until crisp
50g snow peas, blanched
2 tbsp pine nuts, toasted
to serve freshly grated parmesan

pasta with artichokes, prosciutto and pine nuts

COOK pasta to packet instructions.
DRAIN cooked pasta, saving ¼ cup cooking water. Mix reserved cooking water with artichoke spread then toss through pasta until evenly combined. Add prosciutto, snow peas and pine nuts. Accompany with parmesan.
Serves 2

200g quality dried pasta
handful rocket leaves
60 g roasted almonds
1 clove garlic
¼ tsp chilli flakes
zest and juice of ½ lemon
½ tsp salt & grinds of pepper
1 tbsp finely grated parmesan

pasta with rocket and chilli pesto

COOK pasta to packet instructions. Meanwhile, blitz rocket in a food processor with nuts, garlic, chilli, lemon, salt and pepper and parmesan.
DRAIN cooked pasta, saving ¼ cup cooking water.
MIX reserved cooking water with rocket mixture then toss through pasta until evenly combined.
Serves 2

200g dried pasta
handful chopped rocket
2 large tomatoes, diced
120g feta, crumbled
2 tbsp capers
2 tbsp chopped olives
zest and juice of 1 lemon
2 tbsp olive oil

deli pasta

COOK pasta to packet instructions. Meanwhile, combine all other ingredients in a bowl.
DRAIN cooked pasta and toss through sauce.
Serves 2

toss in a pan

Start testing pasta 1-2 minutes before the manufacturer's specified cooking time. Where possible (and this works especially well with liquid sauces such as tomato) drain the pasta with still a couple of minutes cooking time left and finish it in the pan with sauce to absorb flavours.

pasta with courgettes, ricotta and lemon

200g quality dried pasta
2 tbsp olive oil
2 courgettes, thinly sliced
2 cloves garlic, crushed
zest and juice of 1 lemon
100g ricotta, crumbled
3 tbsp grated parmesan
½ tsp salt & grinds pepper
2 tbsp pine nuts, toasted

COOK pasta to packet instructions.
HEAT 1 tbsp of the oil in a large, deep frypan over medium heat and fry courgettes and garlic until softened and lightly browned, 2-3 minutes. Remove from pan and set aside.
DRAIN cooked pasta, saving ¼ cup cooking water.
PLACE pasta and reserved liquid in courgette cooking pan with lemon zest, juice and remaining 1 tbsp oil.
TOSS with tongs to coat pasta evenly. Add courgettes along with all remaining ingredients. Toss and serve.
Serves 2

lemon pasta with peas and prawns

200g quality dried pasta
½ cup cream
1 clove garlic, crushed
2 tomatoes, diced
½ tsp salt & grinds of pepper
180-200g raw prawn meat
100 g frozen peas
zest of 1 lemon
2 tbsp lemon juice
2 tbsp finely chopped parsley

COOK pasta to packet directions.
HEAT cream in a saucepan with garlic, tomatoes and seasonings. Simmer gently for 5 minutes then add prawns, peas and lemon zest and juice.
SIMMER until prawns are cooked through and pink, 3-5 minutes.
ADD parsley and adjust seasonings to taste.
TOSS sauce through cooked pasta and serve.
Serves 2

AL DENTE
Without that toothsome bite that goes by the term 'al dente' pasta is sludgy and dull.
Dried pasta tends to be more robust than fresh and will hold its texture for longer. The key is high-protein durum wheat flour. Check the packet to ensure the pasta you buy is produced with this flour.

take a jar of pasta sauce

PASTA SAUCE ADDITIONS

Simmer pasta sauce with other ingredients to produce a substantial meal.

TUNA, TOMATO AND PEPPER PASTA

Heat 500 ml pasta sauce with 180-200g can tuna, drained, 75 g black olives, 2 sliced roasted red peppers, 2 tbsp chopped basil or
parsley, 1 tbsp capers, 1 tsp chilli flakes, ½ tsp salt and several grinds of pepper. Toss with 500g cooked drained pasta.

Serves 4

CHICKEN, TOMATO AND PEPPER PASTA

Prepare tuna, tomato and pepper sauce (above), replacing tuna with 200g thinly sliced raw chicken. Simmer until chicken is cooked through, about 5 minutes.

Serves 4

Judging by how much aisle space pasta sauces take up in supermarkets these days I am not alone in figuring that a jar of tomato-based pasta sauce is a handy thing. Very handy, in fact, and not just for pasta. See the soups chapter, page 87, for a quick soup base using pasta sauce, and the roasts chapter, page 162, for a pasta sauce base for baked chicken. There are lots of flavour variations available – it's just a matter of choosing one you like. Both the traditional or the basil and tomato varieties provide a base that works with a range of flavour additions.

Two cups (500ml) pasta sauce are quite sufficient for 4-5 serves pasta (400-500g dried pasta). Use less if you are looking for a light pasta coating rather than a sauce.

Once opened, pasta sauce will keep in the fridge for 5-7 days, or can be frozen. Reheated sauce can be heated again.

stir an asian sauce

Rich with the flavours of the tropics, a laksa sauce base offers the starting point for all kinds of satisfying noodle dishes. The sauce can be prepared in advance and will keep for several days in the fridge or can be frozen.

LAKSA FLAVOURS

2 tbsp flavourless oil

2 tsp minced fresh ginger

1 tsp ground turmeric

1 red chilli, seeded and finely chopped, or ½ tsp chilli flakes

2 fresh kaffir lime leaves

zest of 1 lime, finely grated

1 tbsp fish sauce

1 tsp brown sugar

TRADITIONAL LAKSA FLAVOURS

Traditionally laksa contains Vietnamese mint and candlenuts but the sauce is very good without these ingredients.

Laksa can be prepared with or without coconut milk. The non-coconut milk varieties use tamarind to provide a tangy sweet and sour flavour. Substitute ½ cup tamarind concentrate for the coconut cream in the laksa base.

Laksa flavours (see left)

400ml coconut cream

1 litre fish stock or chicken stock

2 tomatoes, cored and chopped

salt & grinds of pepper

malay laksa base

HEAT oil and cook ginger, turmeric and chilli for a few seconds.

ADD all other flavour ingredients, coconut cream, stock and tomatoes and simmer 5 minutes. Season well with salt and pepper. Remove kaffir leaves. Cool, cover and chill for up to 2 days if not using at once, or freeze. Recipe is easily doubled or trebled.

Serves 4-6

Storage Base will keep in the fridge for several days or can be frozen.

½ recipe Malay laksa base

300g cooked rice noodles

6-8 large prawns

2 eggs, hardboiled

½ Lebanese cucumber or ¼ telegraph cucumber

handful bean sprouts

4 tbsp coriander leaves

prawn laksa

ADD prawns to hot laksa base and simmer 5 minutes.

DIVIDE noodles between serving bowls and top with laksa and prawns.

GARNISH with halved eggs, diced cucumber, sprouts and coriander.

Serves 2

½ recipe Malay laksa base

450 g chopped fresh vegetables

150g diced tofu

1 tbsp peanut butter

vegetarian laksa

ADD all ingredients to hot laksa base made with vegetable stock. Simmer until vegetables are tender, 4-8 minutes. Garnish as for prawn laksa, adding 2 tbsp chopped peanuts.

Serves 2

stir-fry rice and noodles

With rice and noodles in the pantry you can always get a quick Asian fix. Fresh noodles will keep in the fridge for over a week. Dried noodles double their weight when cooked.

CHILLI-LIME FLAVOURS

2 tbsp flavourless oil (eg grapeseed)

zest of 1 lime

1 red chilli, finely minced or ½ tsp chilli flakes

1 tsp brown sugar

2 tbsp fish sauce

2 tbsp lime juice

500g cooked or fresh noodles

chilli-lime flavours (left)

100g cooked chicken, sliced

50g snow peas, sliced

125 ml coconut cream

4 tbsp chopped mint or coriander

2 spring onions, very finely sliced

chilli-lime chicken and noodles

IF noodles are fresh place in a sieve and run under cold water to moisten. Drain and place in a frypan with chilli-lime flavours. Stir-fry over medium heat for 1-2 minutes.
ADD remaining ingredients and stir-fry another 2 minutes to fully heat through.

Serves 2

To extend Add 2 cups lightly cooked vegetables, eg broccoli, peppers, mushrooms, and 1 cup bean sprouts.

---

3 tbsp flavourless oil

3 eggs

2 tsp fish sauce

2 tsp soy sauce

2 spring onions, diced

1 carrot, peeled and diced

4 cups cooked rice

100g ham, diced

75 g roasted cashews

125g soy beans or peas

optional 100g diced cooked prawns or chicken, sliced barbecue pork, handful bean sprouts

jumbo fried rice

HEAT 1 tbsp of the oil in a large, heavy pan. Whisk eggs with fish sauce and soy sauce. Pour into pan and swirl to cover base. Cook until set then transfer to a plate.
SLICE cooked egg into strips.
ADD remaining oil to pan and stir-fry spring onions and carrot for 1 minute. Pile rice on top and cook for 2 minutes over medium heat without stirring.
ADD cooked egg, ham, cashews, beans or peas and optional ingredients and stir-fry until heated through, 2-3 minutes.

Serves 2

■ **Tofu Fried Rice**
Omit ham. Dice 100g tofu and mix with 2 tbsp soy sauce and 1 tsp grated fresh ginger. Fry with spring onions and carrot.

■ **Thai-style Fried Rice**
Use chicken instead of ham and serve a fried egg on top. Accompany with Thai sweet chilli dressing (page 128) and wedges of lime.

stir and serve...

couscous

A bowl of flavoursome couscous is the easiest thing in the world to prepare. Start with equal quantities of boiling water or stock and instant couscous and add flavours of your preference. That's it!

125 ml boiling water
zest of 1 lemon
1 tsp salt
½ tsp freshly ground pepper
1 cup couscous

couscous base

PLACE boiling water in a bowl with zest, salt and pepper. Mix in couscous. Stand for 10 minutes, fluff with a fork to separate then add flavourings of your choice. Serve cool or reheat in the microwave or steamer for a few minutes.

Makes 2 cups, serves 4
Storage Prepared couscous will keep in the fridge for 1-2 days.

1 parsnip, 1 kumara and 250g pumpkin, all peeled and cut into chunks
1 red pepper, cut into chunks
2 tbsp oil
1 tsp cumin seeds
1 recipe couscous base
salt & grinds of pepper
2 tbsp sesame seeds

roasted vegetable couscous

PLACE vegetables in a large roasting dish. Mix oil with cumin and toss through vegetables. Spread out in dish and roast at 220°C until golden and tender, about 30 minutes.
TOSS cooked vegetables through couscous base. Season to taste. Garnish with sesame seeds.
Serves 4 as a light meal

1 recipe couscous base
1 cup cooked chickpeas
1 roasted pepper, sliced
½ cup roasted almonds
¼ cup chopped coriander or mint
2 tbsp lemon juice

chickpea and pepper couscous

COMBINE all ingredients. Accompany with harissa (see recipe right) or chermoula dressing (page 18).
Serves 4

HARISSA
Grind 2 tsp toasted coriander seeds and 1 tsp toasted cumin seeds in a mortar and pestle or spice grinder. Add ½ tsp cayenne. Heat 2 tbsp oil and sizzle 4 cloves crushed garlic and 1 tbsp chilli flakes. Place in blender with flesh of 2 roasted red peppers or 1 cup tomato purée and ground spices. Purée until smooth. Spoon into a jar, cover with layer of oil and refrigerate. Harissa will keep for 2-3 weeks in the fridge.
Makes about 300 ml

crack an egg

SOFT-BOILED EGGS

Everyone has a preferred way of doing this and a preferred texture. For me it's a just-set white (nothing clear, thank you) and a creamy yolk. To achieve this I carefully lower room-temperature eggs into a pot of simmering water to cover and set the timer for 4 minutes, then take them out to stand for a minute before lopping off their heads. The longer you leave the egg before you whip the top off, the firmer it will become.

HARD-BOILED EGGS

Simmer eggs for 10 minutes then drain and run under the cold tap. Crack on the bench and remove the shells. Rinse if required.

POACHED EGGS

Bring a pan (preferably non-stick) of water 5-6cm deep to the boil. Add a teaspoon of salt. Crack a fresh egg into a cup. Swirl the water and add egg (it needs to be really fresh or the white will spread out). Simmer gently until white is set. Remove with a slotted spoon.

In the desert island scenario, eggs are the food I couldn't do without. I have thought about this a bit and considered other worthy alternatives – lemons (to flavour all that fish), even chocolate, taking Don Quixote as my cue. But actually man/woman cannot live by love or chocolate alone (well, at least not for extended periods) and if the fish ain't biting, sucking lemons, while a great appetite suppressant, won't put a smile on your face.

No other ingredient exhibits the chameleon-like appetite appeal of eggs, from the unctuous, silky pleasures of raw egg (coating a carbonara or enriching a mayonnaise) to the ethereal mystery of meringue and all the comforting pleasures of boiled, scrambled and fried eggs.

I like to use fresh organic eggs or, at the least, free-range eggs. In flavour terms the egg is an ingredient where you really taste the difference.

An egg's freshness is determined by the amount of air that has seeped through the shell. When first laid an egg has almost no air inside and as a result will sit at the bottom of a bowl of cold water. As it ages and air seeps in, the egg will start to sit up on its end in the water until, when it is rotten, it will float.

Store eggs in the fridge. If a recipe calls for egg yolks, freeze the leftover whites in ice cube trays and use them to glaze a pastry shell. Fresh yolks will keep in the fridge for a couple of days under cover of cold water. Use them to make lemon curd or custard, to put a shine on a pastry crust or for mayonnaise.

whisk an omelette

An omelette is such a simple pleasure and yet one that always satisfies – just the thing for a cosy breakfast in bed or, as Elizabeth David would say, for a solitary meal with a glass of wine.

2 freshest free-range eggs
½ tsp salt & grinds of pepper
1 tbsp butter
2-3 tbsp chopped fresh soft herbs, eg chervil, parsley, basil
1 tsp fresh thyme leaves

french herb omelette

USE a fork to lightly whisk eggs with salt and pepper. HEAT butter in a small frypan over high heat, swirling it around the pan. When it starts to turn light brown pour in egg mixture. Use a fork or spatula to loosen egg as it sets, drawing it from the outside toward the centre until omelette is almost set. Sprinkle with herbs and any additional toppings (see below) and fold in half. Transfer to a serving plate and garnish with extra fresh herbs.
Serves 1

■ **Cheese and Herb Omelette**
Add 2 tbsp grated cheese.
■ **Ham and Herb Omelette**
Sizzle 50g diced ham in the heated butter before adding eggs.
■ **Tomato and Herb Omelette**
Sizzle 1 sliced tomato in heated butter before adding eggs.
■ **Mushroom Omelette**
Sizzle 4 sliced button mushrooms in heated butter before adding eggs.

wake up...
to eggs

Weekends are a great time to lounge about over a leisurely breakfast. Scramble some eggs and fry some crispy bacon to pile on to toast or for a special occasion sandwich in cooked pastry cases. Mix sparkling wine and orange juice or make a bloody mary and call it brunch.

2 rashers bacon
2 cooked pastry cases (page 102)
4 eggs
1 tbsp cream or milk
½ tsp salt & grinds pepper
1 tbsp butter

creamy egg and bacon mille-feuille

Cook bacon in a little oil until crispy. Place in a 125°C oven to keep warm, along with the cooked pastry cases, while you cook the eggs.
Lightly whisk eggs with cream or milk, salt and pepper. Heat butter in a frypan and when it sizzles roll around pan to coat base. Add egg and cook over medium heat using a spatula to draw cooked egg into the centre as it starts to set. Remove from heat when curds are set but still creamy. Split pastry cases and fill with bacon and eggs. Serve at once.

Serves 2

1 tbsp flavourless oil
1 tsp sesame oil
handful bean sprouts
8-10 mushrooms, sliced
2 spring onions, sliced
5 eggs
2 tsp fish sauce
1 tsp soy sauce
grinds of pepper

egg foo yung

HEAT oils in a medium frypan. Add vegetables and stir-fry over medium heat until softened, about 2 minutes.
WHISK eggs with fish sauce, soy sauce and pepper. Pour over vegetables and cook over medium-low heat until egg sets, 5 minutes. Place under preheated grill to lightly brown top. Serve in wedges.

Serves 2-3

SPICED FRIED TOMATOES
Combine 1 tsp brown sugar, 1 tsp curry powder, ½ tsp salt and a generous amount of pepper in a small bowl.
Halve 4 tomatoes and dip into mixture to lightly coat. Fry in a little butter on cut side until starting to soften. These make a good accompaniment to bacon and egg breakfasts, brunch fritters and salads.

Serves 4

feed a crowd ...
with eggs

Take fresh or leftover cooked vegetables, smoked salmon, bacon or whatever flavours you fancy and mix them with eggs for a fabulous frittata. Bake it in the oven or cook it in a frypan. Either way it's satisfying and substantial fuel for breakfast, lunch or dinner.

6-8 large cooked potatoes, diced
250g cooked, drained spinach
150g feta, crumbled
1 red pepper or 2 tomatoes, thinly sliced
12 large eggs
1 tsp salt & grinds pepper
8 tbsp chopped fresh herbs, eg parsley, basil
100g gruyère, grated

potato, spinach and pepper frittata

PREHEAT oven to 180°C. Grease a 32cm x 23cm baking dish with butter or line with baking paper to cover base and sides.
SPREAD potatoes on the base, cover with spinach, sprinkle with feta and top with pepper or tomatoes.
BEAT eggs lightly with salt and pepper. Mix in herbs and pour over vegetables. Sprinkle with cheese.
BAKE until set and lightly golden – 50-60 minutes.
SERVE warm or cool. Accompany with crisp green salad.

Serves 8

Storage Cover cooked frittata and store in the fridge for up to 24 hours. Serve at room temperature or reheat briefly in microwave. Do not freeze.

■ **Asparagus and Smoked Salmon Frittata**
Prepare frittata with 12 eggs and seasonings, adding 200g thinly sliced smoked salmon or flaked hot smoked salmon, 12-16 lightly cooked asparagus spears, zest of 1 lemon, salt and pepper.

■ **Summer Vegetable Frittata**
Prepare frittata with 12 eggs and seasonings, adding 4 tbsp basil pesto, 2 tbsp chopped parsley, 2-3 diced courgettes, 250 g corn kernels, 2 sliced spring onions and 50 g freshly grated parmesan.

FRYPAN FRITTATA
To make frittata in a frypan, whisk eggs in a big mixing bowl with salt and pepper then mix in all other ingredients. Heat oil in a large, heavy frypan and cook mixture over very low heat, lifting cooked egg from base a couple of times to allow raw egg to run underneath. Cook until semi-set, 6-7 minutes, then place under a preheated grill to set the top. Cool in pan.

toast a tortilla

A stash of fresh flour tortillas allows for the construction of quesadillas and a raft of Mexican (or whatever flavour you fancy) wraps. Store tortillas in the freezer for anytime use. The fillings used here are also good for panini or toasted sandwiches or bagels.

2 fresh flour tortillas
1 tbsp tapenade
1 tomato, thinly sliced
25g grated cheddar
garnish handful of basil leaves, shredded

tomato, tapenade and cheese

PLACE 1 tortilla in a heated frypan, spread with tapenade and top with tomato and cheese. Place the other tortilla on top and cook until starting to brown on the base (1-2 minutes) then flip to cook the other side. CUT in wedges to serve and garnish with basil. Or cook a single tortilla with fillings on one side and fold over the other side to cover.
Serves 2

■ **Chicken, Cranberry and Brie**
Spread each tortilla with 2 tbsp cranberry jelly and cover with 4-5 thin slices smoked chicken breast and 50g thinly sliced brie.

■ **Cream Cheese, Smoked Salmon, Pesto and Rocket**
Spread each tortilla with 2 tbsp cream cheese and 1 tbsp pesto. Top with 4-5 slices smoked salmon and a few rocket or spinach leaves.

■ **Duck, Black Bean and Spring Onion**
Spread each tortilla with 1 tbsp black bean sauce and top with 75 g (5 tbsp) chopped roasted duck or chicken meat and 1 finely sliced spring onion.

■ **Mozzarella, Tomato and Basil**
Slice 50-60g fresh mozzarella over tortilla and top with 1 thinly sliced tomato and 8-10 basil leaves. Season with salt and pepper.

TORTILLA WRAPS
A pile of fresh, warm flour tortillas served with various fillings for everyone to help themselves to is a casual, convivial way to entertain. Include shredded lettuce, guacamole, sour cream, grated cheese, sliced cucumber, tomatoes, mushrooms and a hot and spicy mince filling.

soups

One of my favourite winter lunches is a big bowl of bouillabaisse made with fresh fish from the market and served with croutons and rouille, followed by a green salad with ripe pears, crisp-fried prosciutto and a little balsamic dressing tossed through. Add some crusty bread, a platter of cheeses, fresh seasonal fruit and a bottle of good pinot gris and it's a feast, all with minimal kitchen effort. Shortcuts such as ready-made stocks, bottled tomato products, canned coconut cream, pestos and other flavour pastes make fast work of flavoursome soups. If you are feeling utterly unmotivated start with a good-quality commercial soup and tart it up with fresh vegetables, herbs, seafood and the like.

For weekend and holiday lunches or late-night suppers over winter it's hard to beat a steaming bowl of soup. Its warming sustenance delivers a real sense of nourishment.

Smoked chicken and leek potage (page 76)

thicken a chowder...

Start with a base of onions, celery, garlic and herbs cooked gently in butter. A little flour provides thickening power or, if you prefer, use potato or another starchy vegetable to give substance and body. Add fresh ingredients and stock and simmer until tender.

chowder base

50g butter
1 large onion, finely diced
1 celery stalk, diced
1 clove garlic, crushed
2 potatoes, peeled and diced
2 tsp thyme leaves
2 bay leaves
zest of ½ lemon
½ tsp salt & grinds of pepper
2 tbsp flour
500 ml well-flavoured stock
250 ml milk

HEAT butter in a large saucepan with onion, celery, garlic, potatoes, herbs, zest, salt and pepper.
COOK gently until onion softens, about 8 minutes.
MIX in flour and cook over medium heat for 1 minute.
Gradually stir in stock and milk and bring to a simmer.
Simmer until potato is tender, 12-15 minutes.
ADD desired ingredients to chowder base and simmer until cooked through. Adjust seasoning to taste.
Serves 4
Storage Chowder base will keep in the fridge for several days or can be frozen. Recipe can be made in bulk.

boston seafood chowder

1 recipe chowder base
400g drained corn kernels
½ tsp salt & grinds of pepper
300g mixed seafood, or frozen seafood mix
2 tbsp parsley
optional 2-3 tbsp sour cream or cream

HEAT prepared chowder base and and add corn and seafood. Simmer until seafood is cooked, about 5 minutes. Mix in parsley and optional sour cream or cream just before serving.
Serves 4

Add to the chowder base on the previous page to prepare a range of creamy, nourishing, warming soups perfect for winter days.

1 recipe chowder base
1 large leek, thinly sliced, including ⅔ green tops
150g smoked chicken or ham, diced
2 tbsp chopped parsley
125 ml milk or cream

smoked chicken and leek potage

HEAT chowder base. Add leeks and chicken or ham and simmer 10 minutes.
MIX in parsley and milk or cream and serve.
Serves 4

1 recipe chowder base
300g mushrooms, sliced
250g boneless, skinless chicken, very thinly sliced
optional 1 tsp porcini powder
2 tbsp chopped parsley
60 ml cream

chicken and mushroom chowder

HEAT chowder base. Add mushrooms, chicken and porcini powder if using and simmer until cooked through, about 5 minutes.
MIX in parsley and cream and serve.
Serves 4

1 recipe chowder base
2 kumara (300g), peeled and diced 2cm
1 tsp ground cumin
2 tsp green curry paste
garnish 2 tbsp chopped coriander
optional ½ red chilli, finely diced

thai sweet potato soup

HEAT chowder base. Add kumara, cumin and curry paste and simmer until kumara is tender, about 15 minutes.
MIX in coriander and chilli just before serving.
Serves 4

CROÛTONS

Remove the crusts from 4 thick slices of bread. Mix together 125 ml extra virgin olive oil, 1 tsp crushed garlic, 2 tbsp parmesan cheese, 1 tsp dried oregano and ½ tsp salt. Brush over the bread on both sides. Dice the bread into 2cm pieces and spread out on a baking tray. Bake at 150°C until golden and crisp, about 25 minutes. Cool and store in an airtight container.
Makes about 750 ml
Storage Store croûtons in an airtight container. They will keep fresh for several weeks and if they become stale simply heat in a 180°C oven for 5-10 minutes to refresh.

spice up a broth...

From one fragrant, spicy Asian broth you can create a variety of wonderful Asian-style soups such as tom yum, coconutty tom kar, Thai chicken noodle or even mussels with spicy coconut chilli.

SPICY BROTH FLAVOURS
½-1 tsp dried chilli flakes
zest of 1 lime
1 tsp minced lemon grass
2 tbsp fish sauce
optional 2 kaffir lime leaves

spicy asian broth

1 litre well-flavoured chicken stock
300g can straw mushrooms, drained, or 6-8 fresh button mushrooms, quartered
2 tomatoes, cored and diced

PLACE all spicy broth flavour ingredients in a saucepan with stock, mushrooms and tomatoes.
SIMMER 10 minutes. If not using at once, chill or freeze.
Makes 1 litre

seafood tom yum

1 recipe spicy Asian broth
250g prawns or other seafood of choice
4 tbsp fresh lime juice
4 tbsp chopped coriander

PREPARE spicy broth base. Add prawns, calamari or other seafood of choice and simmer until cooked through, about 2-3 minutes.
MIX in lime juice and coriander and serve.
Serves 4

chicken tom yum

1 recipe spicy Asian broth
150g raw chicken, very thinly sliced
4 tbsp fresh lime juice
4 tbsp chopped coriander

PREPARE broth base. Add chicken and simmer until cooked through, 3-4 minutes.
MIX in lime juice and coriander and serve.
Serves 4

Prepare the spicy Asian broth on the previous page as a base for these aromatic meals-in-a-bowl or use a good commercial Asian flavour blend or paste.

1 recipe spicy Asian broth
150 ml coconut cream
1kg fresh mussels, scrubbed clean
4 tbsp chopped coriander

mussels in coconut chilli broth

PREPARE broth base. Add coconut cream and mussels, cover tightly and simmer until mussels open. Discard any that do not open.
MIX in coriander.
Serves 4

FRESH FLAVOURS
If using a commercial blend or paste to prepare these soups, boost the flavour by adding fresh ingredients such as lime zest, coriander, mint and lemon grass.

1 recipe spicy Asian broth
150 ml coconut cream
150g raw chicken, thinly sliced
2 tbsp lime or lemon juice
4 tbsp chopped coriander

chicken tom kar

PREPARE broth base. Add coconut cream and chicken and simmer until chicken is cooked through, 3-4 minutes.
MIX in lime or lemon juice and coriander.
Serves 4

1 recipe spicy Asian broth
150 ml coconut cream
150g chicken, thinly sliced
200g cooked or fresh noodles, eg rice sticks
1 handful bean sprouts
4cm cucumber, sliced thinly
coriander

thai chicken noodle soup

PREPARE spicy soup broth. Add coconut cream and chicken and simmer until chicken is cooked through, 3-4 minutes.
DIVIDE noodles between serving bowls, spoon over soup and garnish with bean sprouts, cucumber and coriander.
Serves 2 as a main course or 4 as a starter

stir in miso

Sachets of commercial miso soup can be used as a base for quickly assembled soups or you can prepare a nourishing broth from scratch using the miso flavours here.

MISO FLAVOURS
2 tbsp miso paste
2 tbsp oyster sauce
1 tbsp fish sauce
1 tbsp minced fresh ginger
1 tbsp soy sauce
zest of ½ orange
1 tsp sesame oil
optional 1 tsp dashi or
Japanese soup stock
powder

1 recipe miso flavours
1 litre hot water
200g boneless skinless
chicken, very thinly sliced
2 heads bok choy or other
Asian greens, sliced
300g cooked noodles
freshly ground pepper
2 spring onions, thinly
sliced

miso chicken and noodle bowl

PLACE miso flavours and water in a large pot and whisk lightly to dissolve miso.
ADD chicken and vegetables, bring to a simmer and cook 3-4 minutes. Mix in cooked noodles and return to a simmer.
SEASON with pepper, mix in spring onions and serve.
Serves 2 as a main course or 4 as a starter
Storage Best served freshly made but can be chilled up to 24 hours.

■ **Miso Salmon and Noodle Bowl**
Replace chicken with 200g fresh boneless skinless salmon, very thinly sliced and 200g diced firm tofu if desired.

1 recipe miso flavours
1 litre water
150-200g tofu, diced
1 large carrot, shredded
2 spring onions, finely
sliced lengthways

miso soup with tofu and carrot

PLACE miso flavours in a pot with water and bring to a simmer. Divide tofu, carrot and spring onions between 2 serving bowls and pour over hot broth.
Serves 4

MISO
Miso is an invaluable seasoning that adds depth and body to soups, sauces and gravies. It keeps in the fridge for months.

choose a cheese

COOKING WITH CHEESE

CHEESE CRISPS

Blend together equal weights of flour, grated sharp cheddar and butter, adding a pinch of salt and cayenne pepper. Roll out like pastry on a floured board, cut into little biscuits and bake at 180°C until golden, about 20 minutes. Store in an airtight container and serve with drinks.

PARMESAN CRUST

Mix equal quantities of breadcrumbs and grated parmesan. Dip chicken or fish into beaten egg then coat in parmesan crumb. Chill until ready to cook. Fry in a little hot butter or bake.

BLUE CHEESE SAUCE

Heat 300 ml cream and stir in 100g crumbled blue cheese until melted. Serve over steak or chicken or grilled figs wrapped in prosciutto.

using and storing cheese

My fridge is seldom without chunks of parmesan or grana padano and pecorino and, in the freezer, free-flow bags of grated cheddar and mozzarella – gutsy cheeses that are invaluable for enlivening flavours in soups. If I am organized there will be a piece of something irresistible such as a small chèvre or unctuous gorgonzola to enjoy with a glass of wine at the end of the day, toss through a salad or serve with fruit after a meal. If you don't have a cool pantry, wrap cheese in waxed paper and store in a sealed container on a plate with a damp cloth underneath to help maintain moisture.

cheese leftovers

Muster those scrappy end bits of cheese in the fridge before they get so dried out or mouldy that you chuck them in the bin. (Actually, mould on cheese is no bad thing and can easily be cut off, unlike the moulds that form on breads, which are carcinogens.) Fire cheese leftovers through the grater on your food processor, bag them up and freeze. No matter if they are a mixture of cheese types or styles, they will still boost flavour and deliver a satisfyingly oozy melt to frittatas, quesadillas, nachos, macaroni cheese, toasted sandwiches and pasta sauces.

chop a tomato...

Whether you start with a bought tomato soup base or the home-made recipes here, you have the basis for some satisfying Mediterranean soups such as minestrone, spicy bean and bouillabaisse.

2 tbsp oil
1 large onion, diced, or 1 large leek, halved lengthways, washed and thinly sliced, including ⅔ green tops
2 cloves garlic, crushed
3 tbsp tomato paste
400g can chopped tomatoes
3 cups chicken or fish stock
2 bay leaves
1 tsp each salt and sugar
several grinds black pepper

tomato soup base

HEAT oil in a saucepan and gently fry onion or leek, garlic and tomato paste until onion softens, about 5 minutes.
ADD tomatoes, stock, bay leaves and seasonings. Simmer 10-15 minutes. Discard bay leaves before serving.
Makes 1.25 litres
Storage Soup base will keep in the fridge for several days or can be frozen.

SHORTCUT TOMATO SOUP BASE
Heat together 500 ml tomato pasta sauce, 375 ml chicken stock and 2 tbsp chopped herbs, eg parsley, basil and chives. Use as a base for any tomato soup.

1 recipe tomato soup base or 1.25 litres shortcut tomato soup base (above right)
250ml white wine
15-20 saffron threads
3 medium potatoes, peeled and diced
1 tsp salt & grinds of pepper
1 tsp sugar
600-800g mixed fresh boneless seafood, sliced
optional 12 whole prawns

bouillabaisse-style soup

HEAT tomato soup base with wine, saffron, potatoes and seasonings and simmer until potatoes are tender, 10-15 minutes.
STIR in seafood, cover and simmer until cooked through, 5-7 minutes, without stirring.
ACCOMPANY with bruschetta spread with rouille.
Serves 4 as a small meal or 6 as a starter

ROUILLE
Mix 125 ml mayonnaise with 2 cloves crushed garlic, ½ tsp smoked paprika and ¼ tsp chilli powder. Add 4 tbsp leftover mashed potato if available.
Makes 185 ml

87

Use the tomato soup base or the shortcut tomato soup base from the previous page to prepare these substantial heartwarming soups.

chickpea minestrone

1 recipe tomato soup base or 1.25 litre shortcut tomato soup base

400g can chickpeas, drained

100g salami, diced

2 courgettes, diced

125g dried pasta shapes

250 ml water

1 tsp salt & grinds pepper

garnish 4 tsp pesto or chopped parsley

4 tbsp grated parmesan

HEAT soup base in a large pot with all other ingredients except garnishes and simmer until pasta is tender, about 15 minutes. Check seasonings and adjust to taste.

MIX in pesto or chopped parsley and grated parmesan.

Serves 4

Storage Soup will keep in the fridge for 2-3 days or can be frozen.

Variations Add other fresh seasonal vegetables as available, eg carrots, parsnips, pumpkin and onion.

moroccan lentil stew

1 recipe tomato soup base or 1.25 litres shortcut tomato soup base

300g lentils

2 peeled and diced potatoes

2 tsp ground cumin

2 tsp ground coriander

1 tsp smoked paprika

½ tsp chilli flakes

HEAT soup base in a large pot with all ingredients until lentils and potatoes are tender, about 20-25 minutes.

Serves 4

spicy bean and sausage soup

1 recipe tomato soup base or 1.25 litres shortcut tomato soup base

2 x 400g cans kidney or white beans, drained

200g chorizo, diced

2 tsp ground cumin

½ tsp chilli flakes or 1 small red chilli, finely chopped

garnish 4 tbsp chopped coriander or parsley

HEAT soup base in a large pot with all other ingredients except garnish and simmer 15 minutes. Serve garnished with coriander or parsley.

Serves 4

Storage Soup will keep in the fridge for 2-3 days or can be frozen.

customize bought soups

GARNISH A SOUP

CHEESE CROÛTONS
Sprinkle rounds of French bread with grated cheese and grill until melted and bubbling. Serve on top of soup.

PASTRY LIDS
Three-quarter fill heatproof ramekins or cups with cooked soup and cover with a lid of pastry, pressing firmly around the edges to adhere. Bake at 200°C until pastry is golden, about 10 minutes.

PESTO AND ROASTED TOMATO
Mix 1-2 tbsp pesto into Mediterranean-style soups and top with a roasted tomato (see page 116).

GREMOLATA
Mix 8 tbsp chopped parsley, 2 cloves crushed garlic and 2 tsp finely chopped lemon zest. Sprinkle gremolata over stews, soups and casseroles.

Start by heating and tasting a little of the soup. Would it benefit from a little chilli? Could it take some substance such as pasta or potatoes or other vegetables, perhaps chopped salami or fresh seafood? Commercially made soups often lack a sense of freshness or zing, and this is your cue to add chopped fresh herbs such as coriander, parsley, mint or basil as well as a little lime, lemon or orange zest.

If the soup is too salty then the addition of potatoes, pasta or rice and a little water or unseasoned stock will help absorb the excess salt. The juice of ½ lemon or a splash of balsamic vinegar can often provide flavour balance.

If the flavour is flat and dull look to spices. A teaspoon or two of ground fennel seeds or ground cumin or coriander seeds provide a quick flavour pick-me-up.

take stock

Keep a supply of good-quality liquid stock in the freezer or pantry for the quick preparation of fresh, flavoursome soups. Simply add flavourings to the stock, grate in fresh vegetables and heat.

750 ml beef stock
1 large fresh beetroot, peeled and grated
1 tbsp sherry
1 tsp soy sauce

beef and beet soup
PLACE all ingredients in a saucepan and simmer for 5 minutes.
Serves 2

750 ml chicken or vegetable stock
200g frozen peas, thawed and mashed or puréed
50g goat's cheese or blue cheese, crumbled
20 mint leaves, finely sliced

minted pea soup
PLACE all ingredients in a saucepan and simmer for 5 minutes.
Serves 2

750 ml chicken or vegetable stock
1 large carrot, peeled and grated
2 tsp grated fresh ginger

ginger carrot soup
PLACE all ingredients in a saucepan and simmer for 5 minutes.
Serves 2

1 onion, finely diced
500g mushrooms, finely chopped
1 tsp porcini powder or 4 crumbled dried mushrooms
375 ml chicken stock
½ tsp salt & grinds of pepper
250 ml white sauce (pg 160)
1 tsp lemon juice

double mushroom soup
PLACE onion and mushrooms in a pot with stock and seasoning. Cover and simmer 10 minutes. Mix in white sauce and lemon juice.
Serves 3-4

STOCK
Fresh, chilled or frozen stocks make the best starting point for soups. It's very easy to make your own – just boil up 3-4 chicken frames for an hour with a couple of onions, a carrot and a few peppercorns in enough water to cover. Strain off the liquid and you have stock. If you prefer to buy stock try to find a brand that is not salted as this can end up making everything you cook taste very salty. As a last resort, use powdered stocks or stock cubes and water. The flavour will not be as complex. If you are a vegetarian, substitute vegetable stocks for beef or chicken stock.

steam open a mussel...
Asian or Italian style

Just the sort of thing to serve around the kitchen table with good friends – messy, finger-licking, comfortable fare that requires the freshest shellfish. Prepare whatever sauce takes your fancy, as mussels are cosy partners to a global palate of flavours.

24-30 live mussels or clams, scrubbed clean
125 ml white wine
500 ml tomato pasta sauce or tomato soup
125 ml cream
4 tbsp chopped parsley or coriander

mussels in tomato broth

PLACE mussels and wine in a large pot, cover tightly and cook over high heat. Remove shellfish as they open and discard any that do not open.

BRING tomato pasta sauce and cream to the boil in a separate pot, or microwave for 3 minutes. Add parsley and the liquid from the mussel pot.

SPOON broth into deep bowls and top with the cooked mussels. Accompany with boiled rice or noodles.

Serves 4

24-30 live mussels
2 stalks lemon grass, bashed
1 tsp green curry paste
1 tsp brown sugar
1 tbsp fish sauce
4-5 thin slices fresh ginger
2-3 cloves garlic, crushed
1-2 small red chillies
125 ml sake or fruity white wine
optional 250 ml coconut cream

spicy mussel pot

SCRUB mussels and place in a large pot with all other ingredients. Cover tightly and cook over high heat, removing the shellfish as they open. Discard any that do not open.

TRANSFER cooked mussels to a serving bowl. If desired add coconut cream to pan liquids and heat through. Discard solids from sauce and pour over cooked mussels.

Serves 4

HANDLING FRESH MUSSELS

Ensure shellfish are from an unpolluted source and that they are spankingly fresh. Discard any mussels that do not close when tapped or run under a cold tap. Scrub and pull off the beards before using. Any mussels that don't open after cooking should also be discarded. Serve mussels as soon as they are cooked.

pastry

In my memory bank of all-time greatest eating pleasures there is quiche and, for entirely different reasons but not far behind, that other old-fashioned classic, bacon and egg pie. Quiche rates for the pure sensual pleasure brought about by too much cream to be decent, quivering tender custard against buttery crisp crust; bacon and egg pie for all those picnics and expeditions made memorable thanks to its robustly portable nature. Egg is the thing that holds many a pie filling together and by its chemistry the more you add and the higher the cooking heat the firmer the filling will be. But pastry offers us more than just filled pies. Think of it as a blank canvas, a bit like a pizza base really, ready and waiting for toppings and a hot oven. Just the smell of pastry cooking is enough to put anyone into a relaxed summer picnic mode.

pack a picnic

Pies like this have loads of appetite appeal and are infinitely useful for informal entertaining as well as being sturdy enough for picnic adventures. You can make them ahead and reheat – just the thing to serve when friends are over watching sport.

3 sheets ready rolled flaky puff pastry (480g rolled thinly)
250g bacon, diced
3 tbsp chopped soft herbs, eg parsley, basil, chives or spring onion tops
12 eggs
1 tsp salt & grinds of pepper

picnic bacon and egg pie

PREHEAT oven to 200°C. Place a flat baking sheet in the oven to heat. Slightly overlap 2 sheets of pastry and press firmly to join. Use a rolling pin to roll pastry a little larger so it will cover the base and 4-5cm up the sides of a large tin (about 25cm x 30cm).

SPRINKLE with bacon, herbs and any other optional additions (see right). Use a fork to lightly whisk eggs with salt and pepper. Pour into pastry shell.

CUT remaining sheet of pastry into thin strips and arrange in a lattice pattern on top. Brush pastry with leftover egg from the mixing bowl or a little milk.

PLACE pie on heated baking sheet and bake 10-12 minutes then reduce temperature to 180°C and cook until golden and pastry is cooked through on the base, a further 40-45 minutes. Serve warm or at room temperature.

Serves 6

Storage Pie is best eaten the day it is made.

OPTIONAL ADDITIONS

Sprinkle extra toppings such as peas, cooked spinach, sliced tomato and sliced cooked potato over bacon. Pour egg over and bake.

SPINACH & SALMON PIE

Sprinkle pastry with 400g fresh salmon cut in 2cm dice. Add 1 cup (250g) cooked drained spinach. Pour egg mixture over and bake as for picnic bacon and egg pie.

vary the filling
or the size

Use the picnic bacon and egg pie recipe on the previous page to make small pies. Or change the filling – spinach and feta, fresh salmon and capers or chicken, brie and mushroom.

2 sheets ready rolled puff pastry (320g rolled thinly)
filling 1 cup (250g) cooked, drained spinach
3 eggs
100g feta or goat's cheese, crumbled
100g cream cheese, softened
½ tsp salt & grinds pepper
topping ½ cup grated mozzarella
2 tbsp grated parmesan or pecorino

spinach and feta pies

Preheat oven to 200°C. Place a flat baking sheet in oven to heat. Cut each sheet of pastry into 4. Spray 8 large (9cm Texas) muffin pans with a little olive oil spray. Place pastry in pans to cover base and sides.
COMBINE filling ingredients. Pour into pastry shells and sprinkle cheese over top.
BAKE for 10-12 minutes then reduce temperature to 180°C and cook until golden and pastry is cooked through on the base, a further 25-30 minutes. Cool 10 minutes before serving.
Serves 4 as a light meal or 6-8 as finger food
Storage Pie is best eaten the day it is made.
Variation Double the recipe for a single large pie and allow an extra 10-15 minutes cooking time for the filling to set.

2 sheets (320g) savoury shortcrust pastry, rolled thinly
1 small cooked chicken or 600g cooked chicken meat
1 cup (250g) cooked, drained spinach
250g sour cream
½ tsp nutmeg
1 egg
salt and pepper
150g brie, sliced thinly

chicken, spinach and brie pie

PREHEAT oven to 200°C. Place a flat baking sheet in the oven to heat. Trim pastry to line the base and sides of a 22cm round spring-form cake tin or pie dish.
CUT chicken meat into roughly 3-4cm dice and sprinkle over pastry base. Spread spinach on top. Blend sour cream, nutmeg, egg and seasonings and pour over. Cover with slices of brie.
PLACE pie on hot baking sheet and bake 10-12 minutes then reduce temperature to 180°C and cook until golden and pastry is cooked through on the base, a further 35-40 minutes. Cool 10 minutes before serving.
Serves 4 as a light meal

roll a sheet of pastry

TO PREPARE OPEN TARTS

Use ready rolled puff pastry or roll out block pastry very thinly (5mm). Cut into rectangles 3cm x 6cm. Cover with topping and bake at 200°C until puffed, 10-12 minutes, then reduce the temperature to 170°C and cook until golden and cooked through, about 15-20 minutes.

TO MAKE PUFF PASTRY SHELLS

Cut a 24cm square of puff pastry into 6 or 8 even rectangles. Place on baking tray and decorate with leftover pieces of pastry. Brush with beaten egg. Bake at 200°C until puffed, 10-12 minutes, then reduce temperature to 170°C and cook until golden and cooked through, about 10 minutes. For filled pastries, use a sharp knife to carefully split in half horizontally. Sandwich with a hot or cold filling.

handling frozen pastry

Keep a stash of flaky and shortcrust pastry in the freezer for speedy assembly of a range of savoury or sweet tarts and pies. Make small tarts for finger food or larger ones for brunch, lunch or supper. Ready rolled pastry is usually a little thick, so roll it on a lightly floured board to around 5mm thickness.

to prepare a cooked pastry case

You may have come across recipes that call for the pastry to be baked blind. This does not require you to hunt out a bandana from a pin the tail on the donkey kit. To bake blind involves cooking an unfilled pastry shell without it rising or collapsing. Line the baking tin with pastry so it covers the base and sides evenly. Cover with baking paper or foil then sprinkle in dry beans or raw rice or ceramic baking beans to weight it down. Bake at 180°C for about 12-15 minutes or until you can lift off the baking paper without it sticking. Reduce temperature to 170°C and cook without the lining until pastry is golden and crisp, about 12-15 minutes. Cool then store in an airtight container if not using at once. Pastry shells will keep for about a week but if they show any signs of staleness, freshen in a 180°C oven for 5-10 minutes.

top a sheet of pastry

Use shortcrust or puff pastry as a base for all kinds of great toppings. You can also use a pizza base, wedges of fresh flour tortillas or sliced bread as a base – simply pile on the toppings and bake until crisp. Try goat's cheese, sliced tomato and pesto, or ham and gruyère.

1 x 24cm square puff pastry,
cut into 8 rectangles
topping 250g mushrooms,
thinly sliced
1 tbsp chopped tarragon or
basil (or 1 tsp dried)
125 ml good-quality
mayonnaise
1 tbsp lemon juice
½ tsp salt & grinds pepper
optional: 2 tbsp pine nuts,
toasted

creamy mushroom tarts

PREHEAT oven to 200°C. Mix all topping ingredients until evenly combined.
PLACE pastry rectangles on a baking tray and place mushroom mixture on top.
BAKE until starting to puff and turn golden, about 12 minutes, then reduce heat to 170°C and cook a further 12-15 minutes until bases are crisp. Serve hot. For a light meal accompany with fresh salad greens.
Makes 8

1 sheet puff pastry, cut into
4 squares
4 large flat mushrooms
4 tsp pesto
juice of ½ lemon
salt & grinds pepper
4 tbsp grated gruyère

roasted mushroom tarts

PREHEAT oven to 200°C. Place pastry squares on a baking tray and top each one with a mushroom, ribbed side up. Scrunch pastry to fit snugly around mushroom.
SPOON a teaspoon of pesto on to each mushroom cap, drizzle with lemon juice and season with salt and pepper. Sprinkle over cheese.
BAKE 10 minutes then reduce heat to 170°C and cook until pastry is golden and cooked through, a further 15-20 minutes. Serve hot or warm.
Serves 4

bake a quiche

Old-fashioned quiche may be but it's gob-smackingly good. You can make these any size – bigger ones will take longer to cook. Be sure the oven is not too hot so the egg retains a delicate custard texture.

26 x 6cm cooked pastry shells
or 12 x 10-12cm pastry shells
(3 sheets savoury shortcrust
pastry)
quiche flavourings (see right)
Quiche Base 3 egg yolks
2 whole eggs
250ml cream
¼ tsp ground nutmeg
1 tsp salt & grinds of pepper
optional 2 tbsp lemon juice

mini quiches

PREHEAT oven to 175°C. Place pastry shells on a baking tray. Divide flavourings (see right) between shells.
WHISK eggs with cream and seasonings. Pour into shells (1 tbsp per mini tart and 2 tbsp per larger tarts).
BAKE until filling is set, about 13 minutes for small tarts and 16 minutes for larger ones.
Makes 26
Storage Cooked quiches will keep in the fridge in a covered container for a couple of days or can be frozen. Reheat in a 160°C oven for 10 minutes.

■ **Family Quiche**
Prepare filling of your choice and pour into a cooked 23-25cm shallow savoury pastry shell. Bake as for mini quiches allowing an extra 10-12 minutes cooking time for the filling to set.

QUICHE FLAVOURINGS

QUICHE LORRAINE
Use 100g cooked finely diced ham and 100g grated gruyère.

SPINACH QUICHE
Use 250 g cooked drained spinach (fresh or frozen) and 8 tbsp freshly grated parmesan

SALMON QUICHE
Use 2 x 225g cans red salmon, drained and flaked, and 4 tbsp chopped fresh herbs, eg basil, parsley, chives.

make a quick lunch

For a quickly assembled lunch, layer the following fillings in a cooked pastry shell or into mini tart shells. To prepare a large cooked pastry shell use 2 sheets of pastry joined together and follow the cooking instructions on page 102.

23cm cooked savoury pastry shell
250 g flavoured cream cheese, eg creamy cheese and herb dip (page 23)
50g (2 handfuls) rocket leaves
100g sliced smoked salmon
2 tsp capers
garnish 2-3 tbsp soft herbs, eg miners lettuce, chives
juice of ½ lemon

smoked salmon and rocket tart

SPREAD cream cheese in cooked pastry shell. Cover with rocket and salmon. Scatter over capers and herbs. Serve drizzled with lemon juice.

Serves 4-6

Variation Prepare as mini tarts to serve as finger food.

½ quantity caramelized onions (page 138)
1 cooked savoury pastry shell approx 35cm x 10cm or 20cm round
200g goat camembert or other goat's cheese, sliced
1 tsp fresh thyme leaves

goat's cheese and caramelized onion galette

PREHEAT oven to 180°C. Spread onions in cooked tart case. Cover with slices of cheese and sprinkle with thyme. Warm in oven for 10-12 minutes until cheese starts to soften and melt. Serve with a crisp green salad.

Serves 4

Variation Make mini tarts to serve as finger food.

salads

Whether to partner a juicy piece of chicken or a wedge of frittata, you need look no further than a bowl of tossed salad leaves. Vary the leaves according to your taste and the season – watercress and rocket offer a good tangy bite, buttercrunch, mache and cos lettuces are sweet, while old-fashioned iceberg offers an unrivalled crunch. Wash and spin greens dry and store in a plastic bag or sealed container in the fridge. Provided they are dry, fresh salad leaves will keep well for up to a week. Make the dressing ahead of time and toss it with the salad just before serving, being sure to only use enough to lightly coat the leaves without any left swimming in the bottom of the bowl.

For main course salads use fresh greens as a base and combine all the elements with a good dressing. Take a less-is-more approach and avoid emptying the contents of your fridge into the salad bowl. A good salad is about balance and texture.

shake a dressing

The French tend to dress their salads individually at the table using oil and vinegar cruets. Showing finesse garnered from generations of good eating, they always seem to end up with just the right quantity of dressing and a perfect balance of flavours.

150 ml extra virgin olive oil
3 tbsp lemon juice
1 tbsp wine vinegar
2 tsp Dijon mustard
1 tsp sugar
½ tsp salt & grinds of pepper
1 clove garlic, crushed

lemon dijon vinaigrette
Shake all ingredients together in a jar.
Makes 200 ml
Storage Dressing will keep in the fridge for a week.

7 tbsp extra virgin olive oil
2 tbsp balsamic vinegar
juice of 1 lemon
1 tsp brown sugar
1 tsp Dijon mustard
½ tsp salt & grinds of pepper

balsamic dressing
Whisk all ingredients, or shake together in a jar.
Makes [1] 125 ml
Storage Dressing will keep in the fridge for over a week.

6 tbsp fresh walnut oil
2 tbsp red wine vinegar
½ tsp Dijon mustard
pinch of sugar
½ tsp salt & grinds of pepper

walnut vinaigrette
Shake all ingredients together in a jar.
Makes 125 ml
Storage Dressing will keep in the fridge for over a week.

toss a salad

SPINACH, BEETS, ALMONDS AND FETA

120g spinach or water-cress leaves, 1 peeled and shredded fresh beetroot (tossed in 1 tbsp olive oil so it doesn't bleed), a handful of toasted almonds and 80g crumbed feta, all tossed together with 4 tbsp lemon Dijon vinaigrette (page 113).

ROCKET, AVOCADO AND BACON

120g rocket leaves, 1 sliced avocado, 3 rashers crispy bacon tossed with ¼ cup balsamic vinaigrette, with shavings of 30g fresh parmesan sprinkled over the top.

LETTUCE, PEAR, BLUE CHEESE AND WALNUT

1 butterhead lettuce, 2 thinly sliced pears, 60-80g crumbled blue cheese, 60g toasted wal-nuts, 6-8 blanched snow peas, 4 tbsp Dijon or wal-nut vinaigrette.

a classic green salad

Something as simple as a bowl of freshest mixed salad greens tossed with a well-balanced dressing is immensely satisfying to consume. The dressing is key as it is the conduit that brings the elements of the salad together. Mustard acts to emulsify the dressing ingredients.

Have freshest salad leaves washed, dried in a salad spinner and chilled in a sealed container in the fridge (or open a bag of prepared salad greens). When ready to serve transfer greens to a large bowl and add vinaigrette or other dressing of your choice a little at a time.

Use your hands or salad servers and toss the salad to coat all the leaves with dressing. There should not be any spare dressing swimming round in the bottom of the bowl.

Transfer to a serving bowl and serve at once.

A fresh, green salad is the basis for all kinds of flavour and texture variations. The trick is not to make them too complicated. If you want a bit more substance in your salad try the combinations on the left. Each will serve 4 people.

roast a tomato

Roasted tomatoes have an intense, rich flavour that goes with just about anything. The juices also produce a terrific dressing. Choose sweet, vine-ripened tomatoes. If removing stems, cut out the tough cores too.

200g fresh mozzarella,
thinly sliced
2 tbsp basil oil
8-12 roasted tomatoes
sprinkle of salt & grinds
of pepper

roast tomatoes with fresh mozzarella and basil oil

TOSS mozzarella with basil oil. Divide between plates with roasted tomatoes and their juices. Season to taste.
Serves 4

4 bruschetta bases
8 tsp creamy feta
4 roasted tomatoes
4 tsp pesto
8-12 rocket leaves

roast tomato bruschetta

SPREAD bruschetta bases with feta using about 2 tsp for each one. Top with a roasted tomato and spoon over a little pesto. Accompany with a few fresh rocket leaves.
Makes 4

600g tomatoes on the vine
or whole single tomatoes
2 tbsp extra virgin olive oil
1 tbsp balsamic vinegar
1 tsp sugar
½ tsp salt & grinds
of pepper

roasted tomatoes

PREHEAT oven to 160°C. Place tomatoes on an oven tray lined with baking paper.
DRIZZLE with olive oil and balsamic vinegar. Sprinkle with sugar, salt and pepper.
ROAST until starting to shrivel – 40 minutes for small tomatoes and about 1 hour for larger tomatoes. Serve at room temperature with cooking juices.
Serves 4
Storage For serving in fresh salads these are best cooked the day they are required, however they may be kept in the fridge for several days.

pick some vegetables

I can't think of a nicer way to enjoy fresh, seasonal vegetables than in salads such as these. Simple assemblies brought together with a flavoursome herb oil, they make a good choice for a light starter or elegant lunch.

400g green beans or asparagus, trimmed
zest of ½ lemon
2 tbsp extra virgin olive oil
1 medium-large fresh beetroot, peeled and shredded
salt & grinds of pepper
150g fresh mozzarella, sliced
4 tbsp basil oil (page 18) or other herb oil
30g roasted almonds

green beans, beets and mozzarella with basil oil

BOIL beans or asparagus in a pot of lightly salted water for 4-5 minutes just until tender. Refresh under cold running water then mix with lemon zest and 1 tbsp of the olive oil.

MIX beetroot with remaining oil and season lightly with salt and pepper. Divide beans between 4 serving plates and top with beets.

TOSS mozzarella with 2 tbsp basil oil and place on top. Scatter over nuts.

DRIZZLE remaining herb oil over and around salad.

Serves 4 as a small plate or lunch dish

3 tbsp extra virgin olive oil
100g prosciutto, finely chopped
120-150g watercress
60g walnuts, toasted
2 pears, quartered, cored and thinly sliced
100g feta, diced
125 ml basil oil (page 18) or other herb oil

watercress, prosciutto, pears and walnuts with marinated feta

HEAT oil and fry prosciutto until crispy. Cool.

TOSS cooled prosciutto and oil through watercress, walnuts and pears. Divide between 4 plates.

TOSS feta with herb oil and divide between salads. Serve at once.

Serves 4

SALTING COOKING WATER

Adding salt to cooking water for vegetables, rice and pasta etc intensifies the flavour.

For vegetables I allow about 1 tsp salt per 1.5 litres of water and for pasta 1 tbsp of salt per 1.5 litres water.

COOKING GREEN VEGETABLES

If you are cooking green vegetables such as broccoli or courgettes to serve as a side dish, add about 125 ml water, a splash of olive oil, a pinch of salt, cover and cook until tender about 4-6 minutes.

119

If you want a salad to take to a party or barbecue you need ingredients that won't wilt or go soggy. The following salads are happily portable, easily extended and go well with seafood, chicken or meat.

cobb salad of corn, avocado and tomato with basil oil

400g whole kernel corn, cooked, or thawed if frozen

4 tomatoes, cored and cut in wedges

1 large just-ripe

avocado, cut in chunks

2 tbsp finely chopped red onion

2 spring onions, thinly sliced

125 ml basil oil (page 18)

½ tsp salt & grinds of pepper

TOSS all ingredients together and season to taste. Serve with meat or poultry.

Serves 4

Storage Prepared salad can be stored in the fridge for up to 2 hours. For longer storage add the avocado at serving time. Return to room temperature before serving.

■ **Chicken Cobb Salad**

SHRED the flesh of 1 cooked chicken or 2 smoked chicken breasts into the salad for a main course.

FRESH CORN
If using fresh corn boil for 3 minutes then drain and cut kernels off the cob with a sharp, heavy knife.

greek-style salad with herb oil

300g cherry tomatoes

2 Lebanese cucumbers, cut in batons

2 red peppers, diced

150g feta, cut in chunks

20 kalamata olives

3 tbsp herb oil, eg mint

2 tbsp lemon juice

½ tsp salt & grinds of pepper

optional 1 tbsp caper berries

TOSS all ingredients together and season to taste.
SERVE with meats, poultry, fish or flatbreads.

Serves 4

peel an avocado

The seductive texture of a just-ripe avocado is hard to beat. Hass and Reed are my favourite varieties, both displaying a creamy flesh and slight nuttiness but none of the oiliness you sometimes get in other avocado varieties.

avocado with vinaigrette

1 just-ripe avocado
4 tbsp balsamic dressing (page 113)
optional: diced cherry tomatoes or basil leaves

SPLIT avocado and remove stone. Dress each half with 2 tbsp balsamic dressing. Diced cherry tomatoes or basil leaves can be added. You can also fill the stone cavity with cooked prawns or crab meat folded through a little mayonnaise.

green goddess dip

1 bunch parsley, stems removed (1 packed cup)
2 cloves garlic, crushed
2 tbsp lemon juice
1 tsp Dijon mustard
flesh of 1 just-ripe avocado
½ tsp salt & grinds of pepper
125 ml flavourless oil, eg grapeseed

BLITZ together parsley, garlic, lemon juice and mustard. Add avocado, salt and pepper and blend until smooth. With motor running add oil in a slow stream until sauce is smooth and creamy.

Makes about 500 ml

Storage Dip will keep in the fridge for 2 days.

avocado and tomato guacamole

2 just-ripe avocados, diced
1 large tomato, finely diced
¼ small onion, finely diced
2 cloves garlic, crushed
1 small red chilli, finely minced
2 tbsp chopped coriander
2 tbsp fresh lime juice
2 tbsp olive oil
1 tsp salt & grinds of pepper

MASH all ingredients together. Accompany with corn chips or pita crisps.

Makes 500 ml

HANDLING AVOCADOS

There is just a day or two between the luscious, creamy, melt-in-the-mouth texture of a perfectly ripe avocado and one that has turned brown and horrid. At perfect ripeness the fruit should give just a little when cradled in the palm of your hand and the flesh should be a soft, creamy green. Do not store avocados in the fridge before they are ripe as this will turn the flesh brown. Once cut they brown quickly so drizzle cut surfaces with lemon juice to prevent discolouration.

fill a salad cup

Such a simple idea, such great taste appeal. You can use cooked chicken or duck, or cook up a tasty ginger sesame meat mixture for the filling. Served at room temperature with a stack of crisp iceberg lettuce leaves, it's just the fix for Friday night drinks or an easy weekend lunch.

300g pork or chicken mince
1 tbsp Thai sweet chilli sauce
1 tsp sesame oil
1 clove garlic, crushed
2 tbsp grated fresh ginger
oil spray
125 ml oyster sauce
2 tbsp chopped coriander
2 spring onions, very finely sliced
to serve 20-30 small, crunchy lettuce leaves

ginger and sesame pork rolls

Mix mince with chilli sauce, sesame oil, garlic and ginger. Lightly spray a large frypan with oil and stir-fry pork over high heat until browned and cooked through, about 5 minutes. Remove from heat, cool and mix in oyster sauce, coriander and spring onions.
Spoon mixture into a serving bowl and accompany with lettuce leaves. Each person spoons a little of the meat mixture into leaves, rolls up and eats.
Serves 4 as a starter or 2 as a main course

■ **Ginger and Sesame Chicken Finger Rolls**
Prepare rolls using chicken mince instead of pork mince

flesh of 1 roasted duck, skin, bones and fat removed, flesh finely sliced or 2 cooked chicken breasts, finely sliced
2 tbsp oyster sauce
2 spring onions, finely shredded
16-20 iceberg lettuce leaves, cut into 6-8cm ovals

roast chicken or duck rolls

MIX duck with oyster sauce and spring onions. Place in a serving bowl. Stack lettuce rounds on a plate and allow people to make their own mini salads, taking a spoon of duck salad and rolling up in a piece of lettuce.
Serves 4
Storage Filling mixture can be prepared and chilled up to 12 hours before serving.

choose the good oil

THE APPEAL OF FAT

Fat carries flavours and gives food mouth-feel. Without it food can often taste very flat and dull (using ingredients such as chillies, citrus, fresh herbs and spices helps overcome this). Whether in the form of oil or butter or margarine, fat is fat and contains roughly the same amount of energy.

WHICH FAT IS BEST

Some sources of fat are better for you than others. Your body will be grateful for oils that are high in monounsaturated fats – read olive oil, avocado oil and rice bran oil. It will be most unhappy if you give it margarine or other processed poly-unsaturated oils with trans fatty acids.

olive oil

Extra virgin olive oil is my preferred cooking oil unless I don't want any flavour, in which case I will opt for grape seed or rice bran oil. For Asian dishes a little sesame oil is often nice, but it burns easily so do not overheat.

Olive oil varies tremendously in quality and flavour. The best oil comes from the first press. If its oleic acid level is less than 1% (and it meets other flavour and chemical standards), this first-pressed oil qualifies as extra virgin. Virgin olive oil has an oleic acid level of 1-3%, while pure olive oil is oil that qualifies as neither virgin nor extra virgin and has been processed further to reduce acidity.

Wherever possible choose extra virgin olive oil over other standards. Commercial supermarket brands of extra virgin olive oil are fine for frying and general cooking. Treat yourself to a bottle of estate-bottled extra virgin olive oil to drizzle over dishes at serving time and where you will be able to taste their special flavours. Avoid pomace olive oils as these are chemically extracted from the dregs of the olives after all the pressed oil has been extracted naturally and often contain undesirable chemical residues.

Smell oil to ensure it is not rancid and store in a cool place. Chilled olive oil may set but it will come back to a liquid consistency when warmed. Do not allow oil to burn or get overheated.

mix and match
salads ...

Salad ingredients lend themselves to a mix and match approach using different dressings. Taking an Asian theme, create a different effect for the following salads using either Thai sweet chilli dressing, soy sesame dressing or wasabi lime mayonnaise. Or buy a good Asian dressing.

200g rare-cooked beef fillet*
100g snow peas or sugar snaps, sliced very thinly lengthways
2 spring onions, sliced very thinly lengthways
½ red onion, sliced very thinly
2 tbsp coriander leaves
2 tbsp Asian dressing

rare beef with green salad garnish

SLICE meat thinly and divide between 2 plates. COMBINE salad ingredients with dressing and pile on top of meat. Drizzle over any extra dressing.

Serves 2

* To cook beef in the piece, heat a little oil in a heavy pan, season meat and brown over high heat for a minute each side. Transfer to a baking tray and roast at 200°C for 8-10 minutes. Stand at least 5 minutes before slicing thinly.

100g snow peas
1 cooked chicken or 4 cooked chicken breasts, flesh shredded into bite-size chunks
2 mangoes, sliced
2 stalks celery, thinly sliced
2 tbsp sesame seeds, toasted
50g roasted cashew nuts
125 ml soy sesame dressing or Thai sweet chilli dressing

chicken with cashews, mango, snow peas and celery

TOSS all ingredients together and serve.

Serves 4

■ **Chermoula Chicken and Mango Salad**
Prepare chicken salad and dress with 1 cup chermoula dressing.

■ **Curried Chicken and Mango Salad**
Prepare chicken salad adding 1 thinly sliced red pepper and dress with 1 cup curry mayonnaise.

ASIAN DRESSINGS

SOY SESAME DRESSING

3 tbsp flavourless oil, eg grapeseed, 4 tbsp rice vinegar, 1 tsp finely minced fresh ginger, 2 tsp sesame oil, 1½ tbsp soy sauce, ½ tsp sugar
Shake all together in a jar.

Makes 125 ml

Storage Dressing will keep in the fridge for a couple of weeks.

THAI SWEET CHILLI DRESSING

4 tbsp Thai sweet chilli sauce, 2 tbsp lime or lemon juice, 2 tbsp fish sauce, zest of 1 lime or lemon
Place all ingredients in a screwtop jar and shake to combine.

Makes 125 ml

Storage Dressing will keep in the fridge for a couple of weeks.

Take the simple ingredients of a slaw and toss with soy sesame dressing or Thai sweet chilli dressing for an appealing change from traditional mayonnaise. Or make a zingy tomato, onion and cucumber salad and dress it in either Asian or classic European mode.

asian slaw

¼ small cabbage (red, Chinese, regular or a mixture), finely shredded

½ telegraph cucumber, cut in small batons

4 tbsp chopped coriander or mint

1 handful bean sprouts

2 spring onions, thinly sliced

4 tbsp chopped roasted peanuts

2 tbsp sesame seeds

5-6 tbsp soy sesame dressing (page 128)

COMBINE all ingredients except dressing. Toss through dressing just before serving. Serve with grilled or barbecued meats.

Serves 4

Storage Undressed salad can be stored in a covered container in the fridge and dressed just before serving.

■ **Sweet Chilli Slaw**
Dress salad with 5-6 tbsp Thai sweet chilli dressing (page 128)

■ **Classic Slaw**
Leave out cucumber and bean sprouts and add 1 grated carrot, 1 stalk celery and ½ finely chopped green pepper. Dress with 125 ml mayonnaise and 1 tbsp lemon juice.

THAI BEEF SALAD
Thinly slice 150-200g rare cooked beef and add to Thai salad.

MOROCCAN BEEF SALAD
Prepare Thai beef salad without dressing. Use 125 ml chermoula dressing (page 18).

thai salad

1 Lebanese cucumber or ⅓ telegraph cucumber, cut in small batons

1 small red onion, halved and finely sliced

2 spring onions, thinly sliced

10-12 cherry tomatoes, halved

4 tbsp each torn mint and coriander

4 tbsp Thai sweet chilli dressing (page 128)

COMBINE all ingredients except dressing. Toss through dressing just before serving. Serve with grilled or barbecued meats.

Serves 2

drizzle a dressing

Using fresh summer produce, have a play with the Mediterranean flavours of garlic, basil, olives, capers, anchovies, parmesan and good-quality olive oil – just right for a laid-back lunch, dinner starter and lazy summer holidays. If you find a good commerical dressing, use it.

200g green beans
220g best-quality canned tuna, drained
12-16 cherry tomatoes
egg and olive dressing
1 hard-boiled egg, diced
6 kalamata olives, pitted and chopped
2 tbsp chopped Italian parsley
2 tbsp lemon dijon vinaigrette (page 113)
1 tsp capers

green bean and tuna salad with egg and olive dressing

BOIL beans for 6-8 minutes. Refresh under cold water. Divide between 2 plates and top with tuna and tomatoes.
MIX dressing ingredients and spoon over salad.
Serves 2

■ **Fresh Tuna Salad**
Use 300g fresh tuna steaks in place of canned tuna. Season tuna lightly with salt and pepper and sear in a hot pan for 1 minute each side. Thiny slice and divide over salad.

1 large head cos lettuce, washed and chopped
12-16 large crostini (page 24)
4 rashers bacon, diced and cooked until crispy
30g parmesan, shaved
½ recipe Caesar dressing

caesar salad

LAYER lettuce, crostini and bacon on 4 serving plates.
SHAVE over parmesan and drizzle with dressing.
Serves 4
Optional additions poached egg, thinly sliced anchovy fillets or sliced grilled chicken.

CAESAR DRESSING
Heat 2 tbsp olive oil and gently fry 4 anchovies and 2 cloves crushed garlic until aromatic, about 2-3 minutes. Remove from heat and mix in 185 ml cream, 2 tbsp parmesan and 2 tsp lemon juice. Season with a little pepper.
Makes 250 ml dressing, enough for 8 servings
Storage Dressing will keep for about 4 days in the fridge.

Use Caesar dressing on a Caesar salad or serve with:
■ Lightly cooked asparagus or green beans.

■ Thinly sliced rare-cooked beef fillet, roasted red peppers, sliced avocado and fresh spinach.

slice and serve...
the freshest raw fish

The freshest fish is glistening, almost translucent, and never dull or podgy. It should spring back to the touch and smell sweetly of the sea. Seafood needs to be kept chilled at all times to maintain freshness, as every hour at room temperature equates to a day's shelf life.

crudo

250-300g freshest tuna loin or other freshest boneless fish
(60-80g per serve)
4 tsp extra virgin olive oil
4 tsp capers
sea salt & grinds of pepper
small handful of fresh soft herbs, eg basil, chervil or Italian parsley
lemon juice and zest

USE a very sharp knife to cut paper-thin slices across the grain of the tuna. Arrange slices on serving plates. Drizzle each serving with 1 tsp olive oil, 1 tsp capers, a sprinkle of sea salt and pepper. Top with a small handful of herbs, a squeeze of lemon juice and zest.
Additions chopped avocado, sliced spring onion, chopped olives, cucumber
Serves 4

raw fish sashimi style

50-60g freshest boneless, skinless fish fillets
Japanese soy sauce
to serve wasabi, lime wedges, pickled ginger
USE a very sharp knife to cut paper-thin slices across the grain of the fillet. Accompany with soy sauce, wasabi, lime wedges and pickled ginger.
Serves 1

latin ceviche

500g freshest raw fish, very thinly sliced
150 ml fresh lemon or lime juice
2-3 tomatoes, sliced
2 thinly sliced spring onions
8 tbsp chopped coriander
1 red chilli finely diced
1 tsp salt & grinds of pepper
MIX fish with lemon juice in a non-corrosive bowl. Cover and chill until flesh turns white, 2-3 hours. Drain off liquids and add remaining ingredients.
Serves 4

take comfort

Childhood nursery foods such as soft-boiled eggs and soldiers (perfect for those days when you just want to keep your head under the covers), gentle grandmotherly soups, melt-in-the-mouth stews and pies that fend off winter lurgies and the cold – such is the stuff of comfort food. It smoothes the rough edges off the day and makes us feel relaxed and at ease.

We tend to equate slow cooking with laborious preparation but here the time is in the cooking, not at the sink. Taking a simple method we can tangent into different flavour profiles – lamb shanks cooked Moroccan-style or à la Provençal, meatloaf like mother used to make, or spicy with Asian flavours. Very simple and yet very satisfying. And extras can be frozen for a quick fix on another busy night.

Bangers and mash with caramelized onions and gravy are the stuff of pure old-fashioned comfort (page 138)

don't cry over an onion

You can buy jars of caramelized onions but bear in mind they are ever so easy to make. If the thought of tearful moments slicing onions is a sticking point, take a slurp of water (or wine) and hold it in your mouth while you chop. No more tears!

6 large onions (preferably red), peeled, halved and cut into thin wedges
375 ml water
4 tbsp brown sugar
4 tbsp balsamic vinegar
2 tbsp olive oil
1 tsp salt & grinds black pepper

caramelized onions

PLACE all ingredients in a large frypan or pot, cover and bring to the boil.
REDUCE heat and simmer gently for 25 minutes, stirring occasionally.
UNCOVER and cook until liquid has evaporated and onions are very soft and dark, about 20-25 minutes.
Makes about 900 ml
Storage Caramelized onions will keep in the fridge for several weeks. They reheat well.

4 best quality sausages, eg Italian fennel and pork
150g peas
350g cooked mash
125 ml caramelized onions
125 ml gravy

bangers and mash with caramelized onions and gravy

COOK sausages in frypan or oven. Boil peas for 2 minutes then drain. Reheat mash and caramelized onions in the microwave for a couple of minutes.
SERVE sausages and peas with hot mash, onions and gravy.
Serves 2

STOP A FRY PAN STICKING

When food starts to stick in the bottom of your frypan (this often happens after you have been cooking eggs), you can re-season the pan quite simply by heating 2-3 tbsp of salt in the dry pan for a few minutes. Wipe out the pan and you will find food no longer sticks.

ADD CARAMELIZED ONIONS TO …

ONION SOUP
Heat 125 ml caramelized onions wiith 500 ml beef stock for a delicious soup or sauce.

CARAMELIZED ONION FRITTATA
Prepare frittata on page 68 using 2 roasted red peppers and 250 ml caramelized onions as the flavourings.

SEE ALSO …
Goat's cheese and caramelized onion galette on page 109.

take it slow...
tender lamb

Every dense muscle cut, from lamb shanks to stewing steak, responds best to slow, wet cooking. All the flavours go in at once and the meat cooks to melt-in-the-mouth succulence.

SUN-DRIED TOMATO FLAVOUR BASE
150g sun-dried tomatoes, chopped
3 cloves garlic, crushed
2 tbsp tomato paste
1 tbsp pesto
zest of 1 lemon
1 tsp each sugar, salt and pepper

4 lamb shanks
1 tsp salt and several grinds black pepper
flavour base (see left)
500 ml beef stock
250 ml white wine
150g chorizo sausages, cut into chunks
2 x 300g cans white beans, drained and rinsed
to finish
150 g podded and peeled broad beans, fresh or frozen
200 g peas, fresh or frozen

lamb shanks with sun-dried tomatoes, beans and chorizo

PREHEAT oven to 220°C. Season shanks liberally and place in a large ovenproof dish or roasting pan that will fit them snugly in a single layer. Bake until lightly browned, about 40 minutes. Drain off fat. (Prepare shanks to this point for all following dishes.)
PLACE shanks back in dish with flavour base ingredients, stock, wine, chorizo and white beans. Reduce oven to 160°C, cover dish tightly and cook until meat is tender, about 3 hours. Ten minutes before serving add broad beans and peas, adjust seasoning to taste and return to oven or cook on the stovetop until greens are tender, 5-10 minutes.
IF making this dish ahead of time, bring it back to the boil before adding the final ingredients.
Serves 4

■ **White Bean and Lamb Stew**
USE 800g-1kg lean diced lamb instead of shanks. Place in a baking dish with all other ingredients. Cover and bake at 160°C for 3 hours.

COOK AHEAD OF TIME
Most slow-cooked meat dishes benefit from being prepared a day or two ahead of time.
Once cooked, allow to cool then chill until ready to reheat. Remove any surface fat before reheating. A dish of lamb shanks for 4 people will take about 40 minutes to reheat in a 180°C oven.

From a single cooking method create a rich lamb stew with Moroccan flavours, give the lamb a French take with white beans, sausage and tomatoes, or bring in spicy Chinese flavours of ginger and star anise. Follow the cooking method on page 140 to prepare these dishes.

MOROCCAN FLAVOUR BASE

1 tbsp tomato paste
1 tbsp minced fresh ginger
3 tsp ground cumin
2 tsp ground coriander
1 tsp fennel seeds
1 tsp salt
½ tsp cayenne pepper
½ tsp black pepper
zest of 1 lemon
2 cinnamon quills

800g-1kg lean lamb, diced 3-4cm
750 ml chicken stock
400g can tomatoes in juice
300g can chickpeas, drained and rinsed
125g dried apricots
garnish 4 tbsp chopped coriander

moroccan lamb with cinnamon and apricots

PREHEAT oven to 160°C. Place lamb in a large baking dish with flavour base at left and all other ingredients. Cover dish tightly and bake until tender, about 3 hours. Serve garnished with coriander.
Serves 4

■ **Moroccan Lamb and Apricot Shanks**

USE 4 lamb shanks in place of diced meat. Cook as for lamb shanks with sun-dried tomatoes, white beans and chorizo (page 140).

**SOY AND CHILLI
FLAVOUR BASE**

2 tbsp brown sugar
2 tbsp soy sauce
1 tbsp rice wine vinegar
4 whole star anise
4 dried chillies
50g fresh ginger, thinly sliced
peel of ½ orange cut with a potato peeler, pith removed
10 cloves garlic, peeled and halved

4 lamb shanks
500 ml tomato juice
250 ml water

lamb shanks with soy, chillies and star anise

BROWN lamb shanks as for recipe on page 140. REDUCE oven temperature to 160°C. Return shanks to baking dish with flavour base at left, tomato juice and water. Cover tightly and cook until tender, about 3 hours.
Serves 4

SPICE MIXES

Buy spices in small amounts from a source that has a rapid turnover. For best flavour toast spices before using – either on a plate in the microwave for 30 seconds or in a pan, until they start to release their essential oils and smell aromatic.

spice it up...
curries

A spicy curry base can be made ahead of time ready to add meat, chicken, seafood or vegetables. You can make the base in bulk and freeze.

RED CURRY FLAVOURS
1 tbsp flavourless oil
3-4 tbsp red curry paste
2 tbsp tomato paste
1 tbsp minced fresh ginger
2 tbsp fish sauce
1 tbsp brown sugar
zest of 1 lime
optional 2 kaffir lime leaves

400ml can coconut cream
750 ml chicken stock
4 cherry tomatoes
optional 200g can bamboo shoot slices, drained and rinsed

red curry sauce

TO make flavour base, heat oil in a large pan and gently fry red curry flavours for a minute or two until they smell aromatic. Add coconut cream, stock, chopped tomatoes and bamboo shoots if using and bring to a simmer. SIMMER 10 minutes.
Makes 1.25 litres, enough for 6 serves
Storage Sauce will keep in the fridge for several days or can be frozen.

■ **Green Curry Sauce**
USE 3-4 tbsp green curry paste (to taste) in place of red curry paste, omit tomato paste and add 1 tbsp minced lemon grass.

1-1.2kg lean diced beef or pork
2 red peppers, thinly sliced
1 recipe red curry base

red beef curry

ADD beef and red peppers to prepared red curry sauce, cover and simmer until very tender, 2½-3 hours.
Serves 6

■ **Green Beef Curry**
PREPARE as above using green curry sauce, omit red peppers and add green beans.

CHOOSING COCONUT CREAM
Canned coconut cream and coconut milk vary widely in quality and the percentage of fat they contain (the fat carries all the flavour). Shake the can to ascertain thickness – the thicker the better. Storage: Check for an expiry date as due to the high fat content coconut cream can go rancid (small cans of Asian coconut cream seem especially prone to rancidity). Leftover coconut cream can be frozen or will keep in the fridge for several days.

It's a good idea to prepare slow-cooked stews with meat and chicken a day or two ahead of time and put them in the fridge. This allows the flavours to develop and, more importantly, brings any fat to the surface where it sets and is easy to remove.

4-6 duck quarters
500 ml curry sauce (page 144)
garnish handful basil leaves
1 small red chilli, finely chopped

baked duck curry
PREHEAT oven to 180°C. Place duck in a baking dish. Pour over red curry (or green curry) sauce and bake until cooked through, about 40-45 minutes.
GARNISH with basil and chilli.
Serves 4-6

1kg mixed "dense" vegetables (eg potatoes, pumpkin, kumara, eggplant)
400g can chickpeas, drained and rinsed
1 recipe red curry sauce (page 144)
200g green vegetables (eg green beans, peas, courgettes)
garnish 4 tbsp chopped coriander
4 tbsp chopped roasted peanuts

red curry of vegetables and chickpeas
ADD "dense" vegetables and chickpeas to curry sauce and simmer 15 minutes. Add green vegetables, stir to combine, cover and simmer gently without stirring until vegetables are cooked through, about 8-10 minutes.
GARNISH with coriander and peanuts.
Serves 4

■ **Green Curry of Vegetables and Chickpeas**
PREPARE as above using green curry sauce.

800g-1kg diced boneless chicken
2 large potatoes, peeled and diced
1 recipe red or green curry sauce (page 144)
garnish 2 spring onions, thinly sliced
4 tbsp chopped coriander

red or green chicken curry
SIMMER chicken and potatoes in curry sauce until cooked through, about 12-15 minutes.
GARNISH with spring onions and coriander.
Serves 6

THAI-STYLE PLAIN COOKED RICE
Place 400g long grain rice in a sieve and rinse under running water. Drain thoroughly and place in a pot with 725 ml water and ½ tsp salt. Bring to the boil, stir well, then cover tightly and reduce heat to lowest setting. Cook for 12 minutes then remove from heat and stand without uncovering for a further 15 minutes. Fluff up with a fork and serve.
Serves 4 generously

mince it

From one mixture you can make meatloaf, meatballs and even barbecue patties. It's a formula to mix and match flavours and cooking styles, prepared just like mother used to make or with an Asian twist.

ASIAN FLAVOUR BASE

1 spring onion, finely chopped
2 cloves garlic, crushed
4cm piece fresh ginger, peeled
zest of 1 lime or lemon
4 tbsp fresh coriander, chopped
2 tbsp fish sauce
½ tsp salt

flavour base (see left)
1kg fresh lean pork or beef mince
1 egg white
2 tart apples, peeled and grated
4 tbsp Thai sweet chilli sauce, plus extra for serving

gingered asian meatballs

HEAT oven to 220°C. Combine all ingredients in a mixing bowl with a wooden spoon (or blitz in a food processor until just combined). Use wet hands to form mixture into large walnut-sized balls. Place on a lined shallow baking tray and cook until lightly browned and cooked through, 10-12 minutes.
Makes 40

ITALIAN FLAVOUR BASE

8 tbsp grated parmesan
4 tbsp parsley, chopped
2 tbsp currants, finely chopped
2 tbsp tomato ketchup
½ tsp rosemary, finely chopped
½ tsp salt

flavour base (see left)
1kg lean pork or beef mince
1 egg white
50g fresh breadcrumbs
4 tbsp milk

italian meatballs

COMBINE all ingredients and prepare and cook as for gingered asian meatballs (above).

meatloaf

Use the mixture from ginger asian meatballs or Italian meatballs (above) and bake as follows:
PREHEAT oven to 180°C. Line a shallow roasting dish with baking paper. Combine all ingredients and press mixture firmly into a loaf tin (about 25cm x 11cm) to shape then unmould on to prepared tray.
BRUSH Asian meatloaf liberally with chilli sauce and Italian meatloaf with tomato ketchup. Bake until juices run clear when loaf is pricked and it feels bouncy when pressed, about 1 hour.
Serves 6-8
Storage Meatloaf will keep in the fridge for 3-4 days.

sizzle a meat sauce

Ask your butcher to mince fresh beef steak rather than buying styrofoam packs. That way you'll know the meat is all just meat and lean to boot.

1 tbsp oil
500g premium beef mince
2 cloves garlic, crushed
4 tbsp tomato paste
500 ml tomato pasta sauce
125 ml red wine
125 ml water
1 bay leaf
½ tsp salt & grinds black pepper
2 tbsp parsley, chopped

a useful meat sauce

HEAT oil in a large deep pan and brown mince with garlic and tomato paste, breaking meat up with a wooden spoon as it browns. Add remaining ingredients, stir and simmer gently 15 minutes, stirring now and then. Check seasoning and adjust to taste.

Makes 1 litre

Storage Sauce will keep in the fridge for 4-5 days or can be frozen.

1 recipe prepared useful meat sauce
1 tsp ground cinnamon
½ tsp ground nutmeg
1 tsp ground allspice
1 large or 2 medium eggplants, thinly sliced
500 ml white sauce (page 160)
2 eggs
8 tbsp grated cheese

moussaka

PREHEAT oven to 180°C. Mix spices through meat sauce. Place half the sauce in a baking dish (about 25cm x 30cm) and cover with half the sliced eggplant.
TOP with remaining meat sauce and then another layer of eggplant.
MIX the white sauce with egg and spread over eggplant. Sprinkle with cheese.
BAKE until golden and bubbling and eggplant is tender, about 1 hour.

Serves 6

QUICK MEAL PUT-TOGETHERS WITH MEAT SAUCE

SIMPLE BOLOGNAISE

Heat meat sauce with 125g black olives and toss through 500g cooked spaghetti. Garnish with 8 tbsp grated parmesan.

SIMPLE BEEF AND BEAN CHILLI

Heat meat sauce with 2 tbsp ground cumin, 1 tsp chilli powder and 2 x 400g cans kidney beans, drained.
At serving time mix in 2 tbsp chopped coriander.

By adding different flavourings to the richly flavoured meat base on the previous page you can create moussaka, stuffed peppers, lasagne, cottage pie, bolognaise sauce, even a racy beef chilli. Another goodie to make in bulk.

1 recipe useful meat sauce (page 151)
125 ml water
1 carrot, peeled and grated
20-30 basil leaves, torn
400g lasagne pasta sheets
375 ml white sauce (page 160)
125 g grated cheese

beef and basil lasagne

PREHEAT oven to 180°C. Make meat sauce, adding water, carrot and basil for the 10 minutes of simmering. Line a casserole dish (about 25cm x 30cm) with a third of the lasagne. Top with half the meat sauce.
COVER with more lasagne, the remaining sauce then another layer of lasagne. Cover with white sauce and sprinkle with cheese.
BAKE until golden and bubbling, about 45 minutes.
Serves 6

1 recipe useful meat sauce (page 151)
1 carrot, peeled and grated
200 g peas
900g mashed potato

cottage pie

PREHEAT oven to 200°C. Simmer meat sauce with carrots for 5 minutes. Mix in peas. Place in a baking dish (about 25cm x 30cm) and top with mashed potato.
BAKE until golden and bubbling, about 30 minutes.
Serves 6

½ recipe useful meat sauce (page 151)
8 tbsp cooked rice or breadcrumbs
2 tbsp chopped herbs, eg parsley
4 tsp ground cumin
½ tsp chilli flakes
zest of 1 lemon
4 large red peppers, halved and cored
topping 80g mozzarella, thinly sliced
2 tbsp pine nuts

spicy stuffed peppers

PREHEAT oven to 180°C. Mix meat sauce with rice or breadcrumbs, herbs, cumin, chilli and zest. Spoon into pepper halves and bake until peppers are soft and filling is bubbling, about 35 minutes. Top with mozzarella and pine nuts and return to oven for 10 minutes.
Serves 4

MINCE AND POTATO TOP PIES
Line large muffin tins with flaky pastry. Three-quarter fill with cold, cooked meat sauce. Top with mashed potato. Place muffin pan on a heated baking tray and bake at 200°C for 15 minutes then reduce heat to 180°C and bake until pastry is cooked through, about 25 minutes.

layer potatoes

Layers of sliced potato are baked with garlic and milk. Add cheese if you like and cream too if you feel indulgent.

POTATO AND ONION GRATIN

Prepare potato gratin layering the potatoes with 2 thinly sliced onions. Pour over milk and top with 125g grated gruyère cheese. Bake as for potato gratin.

JERUSALEM ARTICHOKE GRATIN

Prepare potato gratin, replacing potatoes with 1.2kg scrubbed or peeled Jerusalem artichokes, thinly sliced, and add 125 ml cream. Bake as for potato gratin.

6 large potatoes, peeled and very thinly sliced
4 cloves garlic, crushed
500-625 ml milk
1 tsp salt & grinds pepper
30g butter, cut in small pieces

potato gratin

PREHEAT oven to 180°C. Layer potatoes in a large (25cm x 30cm) shallow baking dish, sprinkling garlic between layers.

WHISK milk with salt and pepper and pour over potatoes. Add more milk if required to almost cover potatoes. Dot with butter.

BAKE until tender and golden, about 50 minutes. Accompany with a crisp green salad and slices of prosciutto, or cooked chicken or red meat.

Serves 6

Storage Gratin can be precooked in the microwave. Cover and microwave for 12 minutes. At serving time bake in the oven for 20 minutes at 200°C.

mash it

- Start with a boiling potato with a high starch content, not a waxy potato.

- Peel potatoes and cut into same-size pieces, cover with cold water, add 1 tsp salt and bring to the boil.

- Simmer until tender, about 15-20 minutes, drain thoroughly and mash to a fine texture. Add seasoning and flavourings of your choice – see over.

You are talking to a mash addict here. Well, I guess there are worse sins, though if I am feeling reckless the amount of butter that goes in could frighten my arteries. Actually, you can get away with using very little butter (or oil) and still produce a very good mash. My mother always made hers with just milk, salt and fine white pepper and it was always light and fluffy.

Mash has many virtues, not the least of which is its ability to be made ahead of time and reheated.

Best of all, leftover mash fries up like a dream for breakfast with bacon and eggs. On this note, if you want to make a really good potato hash, heat a little butter or oil in a heavy frypan, add the cold leftover mash (for bubble and squeak add leftover cooked brussel sprouts or cabbage, or sliced corned beef for a corned beef hash), squish it down in the pan and then – here's the clever trick – pour over 2 table-spoons water. Cover with an anti-splatter guard and cook over medium-high heat until crusty, about 5 minutes, then flip and cook the other side. Adding the water makes the mixture crust beautifully.

mash and mix

I always cook more mash than we will eat at a single meal as it keeps in the fridge for several days. Mash can be used as an instant thickener for soups, mixed into a spicy rouille (page 87), as a topping for pies, or mixed with flavours to produce a tasty savoury cake.

5 large potatoes, peeled and chopped into 3-4cm chunks
2 tbsp butter
4 tbsp milk
½ tsp salt and a good sprinkle white pepper

creamy mash

BOIL potatoes in salted water until tender. Drain thoroughly, return to heat for a minute or two to dry out, then mash with a fork or potato masher or put through a potato ricer. Heat butter and milk for 30 seconds in microwave and add to potatoes along with salt and white pepper.
MASH or beat with a wooden spoon until smooth and creamy, adding more milk if necessary. Do not process in a food processor or it will go gloopy.
Serves 4

2½ cups (600g) mashed potato (can use leftover)
150g fresh salmon, chopped in small pieces
50g feta, crumbled
1 tbsp chopped dill or coriander
1 egg
zest of ½ lemon
½ tsp salt & grinds pepper
1 egg, lightly beaten to glaze

salmon cakes

PREHEAT oven to 220°C. Combine all ingredients (except glaze) in a mixing bowl. Form into 6-8 large balls, place on a lined baking tray and flatten slightly. BRUSH with beaten egg and bake 15 minutes.
Makes 8, serve 1-2 per person

■ Corned Beef Cakes
Prepare as above substituting 150g shredded corned beef for salmon and 1 tbsp chopped parsley for dill. Cook as for salmon cakes.

250-300g boneless skinless smoked fish, flaked
2 hard-boiled eggs, quartered
1 stalk celery, finely diced
375 ml white sauce (page 160)
500g mash, softened with a little milk
olive oil spray

creamy smoked fish pie

PREHEAT oven to 200°C. Place fish, eggs and celery in a small, shallow gratin dish. Spoon over white sauce.
MIX mash with a little milk to a spreadable consistency.
SPREAD over top of dish and run a fork through to create ridges. Spray top with oil spray. Bake until bubbling and golden, about 20 minutes.
Serves 2

MASH VARIATIONS

ROASTED GARLIC MASH
Add 1 tbsp/5 cloves roasted garlic per cup of cooked mash.

BLUE CHEESE MASH
Add 60g crumbled blue cheese per 250g mash.

TRUFFLE MASH
Add 1 tsp truffle oil per 250g mash.

KUMARA MASH
Prepare mash using equal quantities peeled, diced kumara and potato.

PEAR AND PARSNIP MASH
Prepare mash using 3 potatoes and cook with 2 peeled, diced parsnips and 2 peeled, cored and quartered pears.

stir until smooth...
white sauce

With a smooth, creamy white sauce you can have cheese sauce, parsley sauce, mustard sauce, macaroni cheese, fish pie, cauliflower gratin, lasagne, moussaka and a true blue (or maybe that's red, white and blue) croque monsieur.

100g butter
5 tbsp flour
1 litre milk
¾ tsp salt
½ tsp fine white pepper
optional ½ tsp ground nutmeg

white sauce

MELT butter in a heavy pot over medium heat.
ADD flour and stir over heat for a couple of minutes without letting it brown. Gradually add milk, stirring constantly, until sauce is smooth and thickened. Season with salt, pepper and nutmeg and simmer 2-3 minutes.
REMOVE from heat and if not using at once, cover with baking paper to prevent a crust forming on top. Sauce thickens on cooling. Reheat in the microwave and thin with extra milk as required.
Makes 1.6 litres
Storage Sauce will keep in the fridge for 3-4 days. It does not freeze well.

WHITE SAUCE VARIATIONS

PARSLEY SAUCE
Add 2 tbsp chopped parsley per cup of white sauce

CHEESE SAUCE
Add 70g grated cheddar per cup of white sauce

MUSTARD SAUCE
Add 1 tbsp Dijon mustard per 250 ml of white sauce

200g dry macaroni, cooked to packet instructions
375 ml white sauce
185g (1½ cups) tasty cheddar, grated
100g diced ham

macaroni cheese

PREHEAT oven to 220°C. Combine all ingredients and place in an ovenproof dish. Bake until golden and bubbling, about 15 minutes. Serve with a green salad.
Serves 2

■ **Blue Cheese and Prosciutto Macaroni**
Follow recipe for macaroni cheese using 100g blue cheese and 4 slices finely chopped prosciutto fried in 1 tbsp oil until crispy, in place of the cheddar and ham.
■ **Cauliflower Cheese**
Prepare macaroni cheese, replacing pasta with 2 heads cauliflower or 400-500g mixed broccoli and cauliflower, cut into florets and cooked until just tender. Sprinkle with 2 tbsp sliced almonds and bake as above.

simple roasts

Anyone who has walked past a hot chicken rotisserie can testify to the tantalizing aromas that come from roasting. Exposed to the dry heat of a hot oven, skins crisp, flavours caramelize and mouth-watering smells are set loose. Our old hunter/gatherer genes click into gear, setting taste buds aquiver and appetites raging. It's all rather primal and greedy, really.

That said, everyone the world over loves a good roast.

There's something very celebratory about a big joint which calls us to gather, share and enjoy.

Roasting is quite possibly the easiest way to cook – season whatever you have chosen, add crusts or stuffings, then throw it into a hot oven to do its thing.

What you serve with your roast can be fancy or simple. One of my French friends does the best Sunday lunch of roast chicken, french fries and a salad. I will often serve a roast with a salad or a big platter of roasted vegetables and aioli or chermoula dressing. English traditions see mashed spud, gravy and boiled greens.

You don't need to make a fuss. Even French bread and salad greens make happy chicken partners.

start with a roast chook

Pick up a roast chicken on your way home or throw one into the oven for an easy meal. How long your bird will take to cook is a matter of age, size and whether or not it has been grown organically. Organic birds are not pumped with water, so take a little longer to cook.

2 tsp salt, eg flaky sea salt
1 fresh chicken, preferably organic or free range
1 tsp each chopped thyme and rosemary
1 tbsp extra virgin olive oil
1 lemon

salted herbed roast chicken

SPRINKLE salt over chicken, inside and out, and chill for 24 hours.

PREHEAT oven to 200°C. Place chicken, breast side up, on a rack (or on a slice of bread) in a roasting dish lined with baking paper. With your fingers, lift the skin around the neck and loosen the skin from the breast area.

MIX herbs and olive oil and stuff under the skin over breast area.

SQUEEZE over lemon and place the squeezed lemon halves inside chicken cavity. Tuck wings under.

Roast until juices that form inside the cavity by the tail bone are no longer bright red and when you wiggle the drumstick it moves freely, about 50-60 minutes (it is important chicken is fully cooked through).

TAKE from oven, cover with tinfoil and rest for 10 minutes before serving.

Serves 4-6

■ **Classic Roast Chicken**
Omit salting process ahead of cooking and season inside and out when you come to cook the bird. Leave out the herb stuffing under the skin. Add lemon and cook as above.

■ **Chicken with Jus**
Pour 375 ml chicken stock and 125 ml white wine over chicken during last 15 minutes of cooking. Skim off any fat from the surface and mix in the juices from the bird's cavity.

SERVE ROAST CHICKEN WITH

■ A salad of fresh greens, sliced fresh pears, caramelized onions and pine nuts tossed with Dijon vinaigrette

■ French fries and a green salad tossed with avocado, tomato and balsamic dressing

■ Potato gratin and a green salad

■ Mashed potatoes, gravy and lightly cooked green vegetables

■ Roasted vegetables with aioli

■ Chermoula with roast pepper and almond couscous

■ Asian slaw or Caesar salad

sauce it up

The chicken may be native to South-East Asia but when it comes to flavours this bird is a global traveller, as happy in the company of lemon grass, chillies and limes as it is with tomatoes, capers and olives.

LEMON GRASS FLAVOURS

3 tsp finely grated lemon grass

125 ml sweet chilli sauce

125 ml water

2 tbsp fish sauce

zest and juice of 2 limes

½ tbsp minced fresh ginger

3 cloves garlic, crushed

1 tsp sugar

4 chicken thigh quarters
lemon grass flavours (left)

lemon grass & chilli baked chicken

PREHEAT oven to 180°C. Place chicken in a shallow baking dish. Combine lemon grass flavours and pour over. Bake until chicken is cooked through and golden, 45-50 minutes.

Serves 4

■ **Provençal Baked Chicken**

COMBINE 250 ml tomato pasta sauce, 125 ml white wine, 2 red peppers, thinly sliced, 50g black olives (optional), 1 tbsp capers, 2 cloves garlic, 1 tsp salt and ground black pepper. Pour over 4 chicken thigh quarters and bake as above.

■ **Moroccan Baked Chicken**

COMBINE 375 ml tomato pasta sauce, 4 tbsp white wine, 4 tbsp chopped coriander, 2 cloves crushed garlic, 2 tsp ground cumin, 1 tsp brown sugar, 1 tsp chilli powder, 1 tsp minced fresh ginger, ½ tsp paprika, ½ tsp cinnamon, juice and zest of 1 lemon, 1 tsp salt and several grinds black pepper. Pour over 4 chicken thigh quarters and bake as above.

3 cups (300g) sliced fresh vegetables, eg broccoli, red peppers, carrots, courgettes (or 3 cups frozen vegetables, thawed)

125 ml water

1 tbsp minced fresh ginger

1 tbsp oil

pinch salt

250g noodles, cooked to packet directions

ginger vegetables and noodles

PLACE vegetables in a pot with water, ginger, oil and salt. Cover and cook until just tender and liquid has evaporated, 5-6 minutes. Mix in noodles.

DIVIDE between 4 plates and top with chicken and its juices, or serve with other cooked meats.

Serves 4

roast vegetables

Chop a variety of dense vegetables, drizzle with oil and fire into a hot oven. These make a great side dish and are a terrific starting point for vegetarian meals, couscous, pasta or panini.

¼ pumpkin, cut into smallish wedges
2 kumara, peeled and cut into chunks
3 parsnips, peeled and quartered lengthways
3 tbsp extra virgin olive oil
2 tbsp maple syrup
½ tsp salt & grinds of pepper
2 red peppers, cored and quartered
300g green beans or asparagus, trimmed

maple roasted vegetables

PREHEAT oven to 200°C. Toss pumpkin, kumara and parsnips in a bowl with oil, maple syrup, salt and pepper. Spread out in a single layer in a large roasting dish, adding any excess oil and syrup from the bowl. ROAST until almost tender and starting to caramelize, about 40 minutes, turning halfway through cooking and adding peppers and beans or asparagus in the last 15 minutes. A splash (1-2 tsp) of sherry vinegar into the hot roasting pan once vegetables are cooked adds a great flavour.
Serves 6

6 large potatoes, peeled and cut into 4cm chunks
2 tbsp olive oil
2 cloves garlic, crushed
zest of ½ lemon
2 tsp chopped fresh rosemary
1 tbsp flour or semolina or cornmeal
1 tsp salt

crunchy tuscan roast potatoes

PREHEAT oven to 200°C. Place potatoes in a shallow roasting dish and mix through oil, garlic, lemon zest and rosemary. Sprinkle over flour and salt and spread out to a single layer.
BAKE until crispy and golden, about 45 minutes.
Serves 6

4 medium kumara or sweet potatoes
1 tbsp maple syrup or honey
sprinkle of salt

maple baked kumara

PREHEAT oven to 200°C. Halve kumara lengthways and use a small, sharp knife to cut a cross-hatch pattern in cut surfaces. If you are in a hurry, place kumara on a microwave plate, cover and cook on high for 5 minutes. TRANSFER to a roasting dish, brush tops with maple syrup, sprinkle with salt and bake about 20 minutes (or about 40 minutes if not microwaving first), until tender and lightly golden.
Serves 4-6

SERVING ROASTED VEGETABLES
A platter of roasted vegetables provides the starting point for all kinds of good eating.

■ Serve roasted vegetables with aioli as a vegetarian platter or to accompany roasted or grilled meats.

■ Toss cooled roasted vegetables through rocket or baby spinach leaves with roasted almonds.

■ Drizzle roasted vegetables with chermoula dressing.

■ Fill panini with roasted vegetables or pile them on to a cooked pizza base. Cover with grated mozzarella and heat through.

■ Toss roasted vegetables through prepared couscous or pasta with a little chermoula dressing or harissa.

go fish

Most people over-cook fish and so only ever know it as dry. Here, cooked in a sauce, the fish remains succulent and moist. Always check fish for bones by running your fingers over the fillets and remove any with sterilized pliers.

2 medium fennel bulbs, halved and thinly sliced lengthways
2 courgettes, halved lengthways and thinly sliced
200g cherry tomatoes, halved
3 tbsp extra virgin olive oil
4 fillets hapuku (groper) or blue nose, about 160-180g each
125 ml fruity white wine
125 ml tomato purée
1 tbsp pesto or basil oil
1 tsp sugar
1 tsp salt & grinds of pepper
garnish basil leaves

baked hapuku with fennel, cherry tomatoes and courgettes

PREHEAT oven to 200°C. Place fennel, courgettes and tomatoes in a roasting dish with oil. Spread out evenly and bake for 20 minutes (dish can be cooked in advance to this point). Or cover and microwave for 5 minutes.
ARRANGE fish on top of vegetables. Combine wine, tomato purée, pesto or basil oil and seasonings and pour over fish.
BAKE until fish is cooked through, 10-12 minutes. Serve fish with vegetables and juices, garnished with basil leaves.
Serves 4

■ **Greek Baked Fish**
Omit fennel from dish and add 50g black olives and 2 tbsp capers with tomatoes and wine. Garnish with mint.
■ **Baked Chicken with Fennel, Tomatoes and Courgettes**
Prepare dish using chicken breasts instead of fish, allowing 25-30 minutes for them to cook through.

4 tbsp lemon juice
1 tbsp crushed garlic
1 tsp each salt and ground black pepper
4 thick boneless fish fillets (at least 1.5cm thick)
125 ml cream
1 tsp each prepared mustard, garam masala and turmeric
½ tsp chilli flakes
garnish coriander

indian spiced baked fish

COMBINE lemon juice, garlic, salt and pepper and mix through fish. Leave to marinate in the fridge for 30 minutes. Combine cream, mustard, spices and chilli and add to fish, mixing well. (At this stage the fish can be marinated in the fridge for longer if desired.)
PREHEAT oven to 220°C. Place fish on a baking tray, spoon over marinade and bake until fish shows no resistance when pressed, 6-8 minutes. Serve with sauce. Garnish with coriander.
Serves 4

flash under the grill fish

Grilling or roasting fish in a very hot oven produces a succulent result in minutes. It's a great treatment for dense, meaty fish such as salmon, monkfish or hapuku. If you are worried about timing, slightly undercook the fish and reheat for a minute or two when ready to serve.

4 boneless skinless salmon
fillets (120-150g each)
Miso Glaze
2 tbsp water
1½ tbsp white miso
2 tsp brown sugar
1 tsp soy sauce
1 tsp sesame oil

miso-glazed salmon

PREHEAT grill to high. Place salmon on a baking tray lined with baking paper (for easy washing up). Combine miso glaze ingredients and spread over salmon.
GRILL fish 8-10cm from heat source for about 5 minutes without turning until lightly glazed and just cooked (salmon should 'give' when gently pressed). Accompany with rice and Asian slaw.
Serves 4

TO FLASH-ROAST FISH

Preheat oven to 220°C fan bake and cook fish until it is no longer translucent in the centre and 'gives' when lightly pressed in the thickest part, about 8 minutes.

Chilli Lime Glaze
4 tbsp sweet chilli sauce
2 tbsp lime juice
zest of 1 lime

chilli lime glazed fish

TOP 4 fillets of boneless fish with chilli lime glaze and grill as above or flash roast.
Serves 4

TOPPINGS FOR FISH

- Tapenade

- Salsa verde

Basil Topping
4 tbsp basil oil
zest of 1 lemon
½ tsp salt & grinds of pepper

basil grilled salmon

TOP 4 fillets boneless fish with combined basil topping ingredients and grill as above or flash roast.
Serves 4

- Pesto

- Teriyaki glaze

- Oyster sauce mixed with a little grated fresh ginger

- Chermoula dressing

- Wasabi butter

glaze and crumb

Select meat from a butcher you trust. Always allow some extra time for the meat to rest after it has been cooked as this allows juices to disperse evenly and the meat to tenderize.

2 lamb racks, trimmed and cut into sections of 3-4 ribs
Chilli Mint Glaze
2 tbsp Thai sweet chilli sauce
2 tbsp chopped mint leaves
2 tbsp fish sauce
1 tbsp olive oil
2 cloves garlic, crushed
½ tsp salt & grinds black pepper

roast lamb rack with chilli mint glaze

COMBINE glaze ingredients and mix through lamb. Chill for at least 30 minutes or up to 12 hours.
PREHEAT oven to 220°C. Place lamb in a shallow roasting dish and bake until done to your liking, about 15-20 minutes.
STAND meat for 5 minutes before serving.
Serves 4-5

1 tbsp chopped oregano
1 tbsp chopped mint
2 cloves garlic, crushed
zest of 1 lemon
1 egg white, lightly whisked

roast lamb with garlic herb crust

COMBINE herbs, garlic and lemon zest in a small bowl. Brush lamb with egg white then roll in garlic herb mixture to coat. Roast as above.

2 tbsp grainy mustard
1 tbsp liquid honey
1 tsp fresh chopped rosemary

roast lamb with mustard crust

COMBINE ingredients and spread over lamb. Roast as above.

whole roasted leg of lamb

PREHEAT oven to 180°C. Place a 1.3-1.5kg carvery roast of lamb in a roasting dish and spread with toppings or crust of your choice, or simply season with salt and pepper.
ROAST 1-1¼ hours or until cooked to your liking (I think it is nicest served slightly rare). Remove meat from oven, cover to keep warm and rest for 10 minutes. If you prefer meat to be slow-cooked and falling off the bone, roast in a covered roasting dish at 150°C for about 3½ hours or until very tender.
Serves 6-8

lick your fingers...
juicy ribs

Finger-licking ribs make good food for easy company. Sticky, caramelized sauces are a nightmare to wash off, so this is a very good time to line the roasting dish with baking paper. Commercial sauces offer a good starting point for a range of terrific glazes.

1.5kg pork spare ribs
hoisin honey marinade
2 tbsp liquid honey
2 tbsp hoisin sauce
2 tbsp soy sauce

hoisin honey ribs

CUT ribs into serving pieces (about 2-3 ribs wide) and place in a roasting pan. Combine marinade ingredients and pour over. If you want a stronger flavour, marinate the ribs in a clean plastic bag or bowl for a few hours or overnight. Spread ribs out in a roasting dish and bake at 180°C, turning a couple of times during cooking, until golden and tender, about 40 minutes.

Serves 6

1.5kg pork spare ribs
Black Jack Marinade
3 tbsp tomato ketchup
3 tbsp worcester sauce
1 tbsp rice vinegar
2 tbsp brown sugar
1 tsp Dijon mustard
½ tsp chilli flakes
1 tsp instant coffee powder
½ tsp salt

black jack ribs

COMBINE marinade ingredients and pour over ribs. Bake as above for hoisin honey ribs.

Serves 6

1.5kg pork spare ribs
Chilli Ginger Marinade
5 tbsp sweet chilli sauce
2 tbsp fish sauce
1 tbsp minced fresh ginger
3 cloves garlic, crushed

chilli ginger ribs

COMBINE marinade ingredients and pour over ribs. Bake as for hoisin honey ribs. GARNISH with finely chopped fresh red chilli and garlic.

Serves 6

desserts

The sweet tooth has many temptations. For some it is the melting seduction of chocolate, for others a crisp buttery sweet pastry, the crunch of dough offset against tart fruit and a film of sugar glaze. Or it might be the dreamy quality of a chilled fruit cream or ice cream that arouses the taste buds.

There are few among us who eschew a little sweetness, unless for reasons of ill health, as sugar is the first taste we recognize (almost from birth). Salt, on the other hand, doesn't register until about the age of four months. These days we end up eating a lot more sugar than we imagine as virtually every processed food contains added sugar. The low blood sugar state that we get into from eating sugar actually makes us crave more.

Which makes dessert a good thing to cook from scratch. Then at least you can choose the ingredients and decide between something healthy such as fruit or something indulgent like a wickedly creamy chocolate mousse.

Balance, after all, is everything.

pick fresh fruit
and a fragrant syrup

A platter of fresh fruit is my dessert of choice on an everyday basis. With clean, fresh flavours and a pique of sweetness, fruit satisfies our after-dinner palates. A simple vanilla syrup, which will keep for ages in the fridge, adds a finishing touch that makes the simplest fruit bowl seem like a treat.

250 ml water
185g sugar
2 vanilla pods, split lengthways, or 2 tsp pure vanilla extract
zest of ½ lemon

vanilla syrup

HEAT sugar and water over medium heat, stirring occasionally, until sugar dissolves. Add split vanilla pods and lemon zest. Simmer gently for 10 minutes. Cool before using.
To serve, spoon a little syrup over sliced fresh fruits.
Makes 250 ml
Storage Syrup will keep in the fridge for months.

■ **Amaretto Syrup**
Add 4 tbsp Amaretto to syrup.
■ **Ginger Syrup**
Use 3 tbsp finely chopped fresh ginger in place of vanilla.

6 kiwifruit, peeled and sliced
1 ripe green melon, peeled, seeded and sliced
small bunch green grapes
1 punnet strawberries, hulled and sliced

fruit salad with vanilla syrup

PLACE fruit in a serving bowl and drizzle over 5 tbsp syrup.

■ **Watermelon and Blueberries with Vanilla Syrup**
PEEL a wedge of chilled, ripe watermelon and cut into large dice.
PLACE in serving bowl with some blueberries and drizzle over a little vanilla syrup.

glaze with toffee...
or syrup

Sugar brings out the juices in fruit, allowing it to create its own syrup. This works particularly well with tamarillos, citrus, stone fruits and soft berry fruits. Choose seasonally available fruit for these treatments.

250g sugar
85 ml water
1 tbsp lemon juice
to serve 6 oranges, peeled and sliced
2 kiwifruit, peeled and sliced

toffee-glazed fruit

PLACE sugar, water and lemon juice in a heavy frypan over high heat, swirling pan to distribute heat evenly. COOK until mixture forms a rich golden caramel, about 10 minutes. Pour hot caramel over sliced fruit.
Makes enough for 6 serves

6 tamarillos or other fresh sliced fruits
5 tbsp sugar

tamarillos in syrup

PRICK tamarillos in a few places with a sharp knife. Place in a heatproof bowl and pour over boiling water to cover. Stand 10 minutes then peel off skins.
SLICE each fruit into 5-6 slices. Place in a bowl and mix through sugar. Stand 1 hour (or up to 48 hours in the fridge). Serve with juices.
Serves 4-6

PASSIONFRUIT AS A SAUCE
Passionfruit provides a tangy yet tropical flavour that goes well with all kinds of fruits. Drizzle passionfruit pulp over pears, peaches, strawberries, papaya, melons, kiwifruit, apples, mangos or bananas. It's a delicious dessert and so simple. Add a squeeze of lime juice if you like.

TAMARILLO JELLY
Prepare tamarillos in syrup (left). Strain off juice and measure, making up to 250 ml with cold water. Mix 1 packet jelly crystals with 250 ml boiling water, stir until dissolved then mix in tamarillo juice. Put tamarillos in a serving bowl and pour over jelly mixture. Chill until set, about 3 hours. Jellies will keep covered in the fridge for a couple of days.
Serves 4-6

brown under a hot grill

Coat sliced fresh fruits with sugar and brown them under a grill. Or mix custard with cream and rum, pour over fruit and grill. Either option delivers a fresh fruit fix with that particular pleasure of caramelized sugars – sweetness with just a hint of bitterness.

grilled fruits

½ pineapple, peeled, halved, cored and cut in 2-3cm slices
4 stonefruit (eg peaches, plums), halved and stoned
2 tsp rum, brandy or orange juice
3 tbsp brown sugar

DIP sliced fruits into rum or brandy or orange juice to moisten cut surfaces then dip into brown sugar.
PLACE fruit sugared side up in a shallow baking dish. Cook under a preheated grill until bubbling and starting to brown, about 8-10 minutes.
ACCOMPANY with custard or vanilla syrup (page 180).
Serves 4

speedy rum sabayon topping for fruit

4 tbsp commercial custard
125 ml cream
1 tbsp rum
½ pineapple, peeled, halved, cored and cut into 2-3cm slices
4 ripe stone fruit, quartered and stoned or 4 kiwifruit, peeled and sliced
1-3 tbsp sugar

COMBINE custard, cream and rum. Chill until needed.
PLACE fruit in a shallow baking dish, spoon over sabayon and sprinkle with sugar.
GRILL until sabayon just starts to turn brown, about 3-4 minutes.
Serves 4

intensify fruit flavours

4 tart apples, eg Granny Smith
4 pitted dates, chopped
2 tsp chopped walnuts or
hazelnuts
4 tsp brown sugar
1 tsp ground cinnamon
½ tsp ground cloves
125 ml maple syrup
125 ml water
4 tsp butter

maple baked apples

REMOVE cores from apples in a neat plug. Use a paring knife to enlarge cavity to 2.5cm diameter. Score the skin around the circumference of each apple with a sharp knife (this allows them to split neatly around the middle when they cook).
COMBINE dates, nuts, sugar, cinnamon and cloves. Stuff mixture into apples and place them in a shallow baking dish.
PREHEAT oven to 180°C. Pour combined maple syrup and water over apples. Dot with butter and bake until apples are wrinkly and soft and starting to puff, about 50-60 minutes.
Serves 4

■ Apricot and Hazelnut Baked Apples
Use 4 dried apricots and 2 tsp chopped hazelnuts in place of dates and walnuts.

500 ml water
200-250g sugar
2 cinnamon sticks
1 tsp vanilla extract
4 whole cardamom pods
zest of 1 lemon
8 dried apricots
8-10 dried pitted prunes
8-12 firm but ripe stone fruit,
eg nectarines, peaches,
apricots
4 pears, peeled, stems intact

arabian poached stone fruits

PLACE water, sugar, cinnamon, vanilla, cardamom and lemon zest in a saucepan and bring to a simmer, stirring occasionally. Add apricots and prunes and simmer 5 minutes.
ADD fresh fruit to syrup and cook on a very low simmer until tender, about 10-15 minutes depending on fruit size. Accompany with yoghurt.
Serves 6-8
Storage Fruit will keep in syrup for up to a week. Excess syrup can be stored in the fridge in a covered container for over a week and used to cook more fruit.

start with good-quality
vanilla ice cream

With ice cream, as with most things in life, you get what you pay for. Products called ice cream can be made with chicken fat (truly!) and packed with artificial flavours and colours. Start with the best-quality creamy ice cream and use as a base for inspired flavour additions.

150g currants
4 tbsp Amaretto or rum or other liqueur
2 litres premium vanilla ice cream
150g finely chopped glacé pineapple
zest of 1 lemon
125g unsalted pistachio nuts
125g fresh or frozen raspberries

cassata

MIX currants with Amaretto or rum. Stand while preparing other ingredients.
SCOOP ice cream into a large bowl and microwave for 40-60 seconds or leave to soften on bench for 10 minutes. Work with a heavy spoon to soften just enough for ingredients to be mixed through (do not allow to thaw fully).
ADD all other ingredients and work quickly to combine evenly. Return mixture to freezer container or individual moulds, cover and freeze for at least 4 hours.
SERVE in slices or scoops. If desired, garnish with diced pistachios and spoon around vanilla syrup (page 180) or maple syrup.
Makes 2¼ litres, serves 8-10
Storage Cassata will keep in the freezer for up to 2 months. Do not refreeze if melted.

kahlua affogato

PREPARE 400ml strong espresso coffee. Stir in 4 tbsp Kahlua, Grand Marnier, Amaretto or other liqueur of your choice. Scoop 4 servings of good-quality vanilla ice cream into serving bowls. Serve a small shot of the hot, boozy espresso on the side for each diner to pour over their ice cream.
Variation Garnish ice cream with chopped candied nuts or fruits.

ICE CREAM FLAVOURS

Mix 4 big scoops (500ml) vanilla ice cream with the following flavours and refreeze for a few hours until firm.

COCONUT LEMON ICE CREAM

6 tbsp lemon curd (page 196 or buy) and 4 tbsp coarse thread coconut, toasted.

GREEN TEA AND GINGER ICE CREAM

3 tsp green tea powder and 4 tbsp finely chopped glacé ginger

ice cream brownie slice

1 chocolate brownie (6cm x 8cm), 1 slice vanilla ice cream,
1-2 tbsp decadent chocolate sauce (page 208)
SLICE brownie in half horizontally and make into a
sandwich with the ice cream. Store in the freezer until
ready to serve. Serve with warmed chocolate sauce.
Serves 1
Storage Prepared ice cream brownies will keep in a
covered container in the freezer for several weeks.

■ **Ginger Ice Cream Slice**
Sandwich ice cream between slices of gingerbread and
store in the freezer.

pan-fried bananas in caramel syrup

8 small finger bananas or 4 regular bananas, peeled,
3 tbsp butter, 3 tbsp brown sugar, 125 ml orange juice
HEAT butter and sugar in a large frypan until sizzling.
Add bananas (if using regular bananas cut them in half)
and fry until lightly browned, about 2 minutes on each
side. Add orange juice and simmer 2 minutes. Serve
bananas with their syrup.
Serves 4

■ **Pan-fried Bananas with Lychees and Passionfruit**
Add a can of drained lychees and the flesh of 2-3
passionfruit.
■ **Pan-fried Pineapple in Caramel Syrup**
Use 4-6 slices fresh pineapple, cut in wedges, instead of
bananas.

espresso granita

375 ml very strong hot coffee, 250g sugar, 2 tbsp liqueur (optional)

MIX coffee with sugar until sugar dissolves. Stir in liqueur if using. Pour into a shallow tray about 30cm x 18cm and freeze until slushy, about 2 hours.

STIR with a fork, breaking up icy lumps, and freeze until firm. To serve, work a fork or spoon across the surface to shave off a fine ice, and scoop into serving glasses.

(If mixture is very hard turn on to a chopping board and chop, then crush with a fork.)

Serves 6

Storage Granita will keep for several weeks in a covered container in the freezer. Break up just before serving.

blueberry sauce

500g (4 cups) fresh or frozen blueberries, 125g sugar, 2 tbsp lemon juice, 1 tsp cornflour, 1 tsp vanilla extract

PLACE berries and sugar in a microwave-proof bowl, cover and cook on high for 5 minutes. Or bring to the boil in a saucepan on the stove.

MIX lemon juice and cornflour to a paste and stir into hot berries. Cook until lightly thickened, about 1 minute.

SERVE with vanilla ice cream, or use as a filling for crêpes (page 199) or crumble (page 200) or fruit sponge (page 206).

Makes 2¼ cups

Storage Sauce will keep in the fridge for up to a week. Reheat to serve.

whip it

ETON MESS
Whip 300 ml of chilled cream and combine with 250g fresh raspberries and 120g crumbled meringues. Drizzle with 250 ml raspberry coulis. Chill until ready to serve.
Serves 6

BROWN SUGAR MASCARPONE AND STRAWBERRIES
Prepare brown sugar mascarpone (page 211) and serve with fresh strawberries for a quick, simple dessert.
Serves 4

CARAMEL CRÈME FRAÎCHE FRUITS
Place 250g blackberries or boysenberries in a shallow baking dish. Spread over 250 ml crème fraîche. Sprinkle with 125g brown sugar. Chill for at least 1 hour. Serve cold or grill until cream melts.
Serves 4

whipping cream

Everything about whipped cream needs to be cold – the bowl, the beater, the cream, even the room you are working in. You will never get silky whipped cream if anything is warm (above 32°C air temperature and the cream will start to separate). Once prepared, cream needs to be covered tightly and kept in the fridge. It's easy to over-whip cream so that it no longer forms peaks but instead sits in the bowl, clumpy and clod-like. If you do over-whip cream, and provided you have not got to the stage of making butter, gently fold in more runny cream until you get back to a smooth texture. When combining cream with other ingredients ensure they are cool, as adding anything warm to whipped cream will break it down. If the cream won't whip it may not contain enough fat – at least 30% fat is required to produce firmly whipped cream.

mascarpone

Much richer than cream with a fat content of up to 65%, mascarpone is a soft, very lightly fermented cheese made with cream and a little tartaric acid. In its absence you can mix cream cheese with cream until it is thick and smooth.

crème fraîche

This unctuous, slightly sour cultured cream is a terrific dessert partner. It is easily made by mixing 3 parts cream to 1 part plain yoghurt or buttermilk, covering and leaving it somewhere warm to sit for at least 12 hours or until thick. Store in the fridge, where it will keep for a couple of weeks.

fold into
whipped cream...

Decadence lurks in desserts of whipped cream folded with chilled fruit purées – fools all of them, if you'll pardon the pun. Or make the classic English syllabub, a divine dessert to serve with fresh berries or fruit tarts.

500g raspberries, fresh or thawed frozen, or strawberries, hulled
3 tbsp icing sugar
2 tsp lemon juice
300 ml cream
optional 125 ml creamy unsweetened yoghurt
garnish fresh or frozen berries

berry fool
PURÉE berries with 2 tbsp icing sugar and lemon juice. Beat cream with 1 tbsp icing sugar until soft peaks form. Fold in yoghurt if using.
FOLD in half the puréed berries. Divide a third of the berry mixture between 6 serving glasses and top with half of the cream. Repeat in layers to fill glasses.
GARNISH with berries. Serve at once or cover and chill until ready to serve.
Serves 6
Storage Prepared fool can be covered and kept in the fridge for up to 6 hours.

RASPBERRY COULIS
Purée 250 g raspberries (fresh or thawed frozen) with 6 tbsp icing sugar. Strain through a sieve to remove pips.
Stored covered in the fridge, it will keep for 3-4 days. Use as a dessert sauce or fold through whipped cream for a raspberry fool.
Makes 425 ml

100g chopped dried apricots
185 ml orange juice
2 tbsp sugar
300 ml chilled cream

apricot fool
PLACE apricots, orange juice and sugar in a heatproof bowl. Cover and microwave on high for 5 minutes. PURÉE and chill. (Purée will keep for several days in the fridge or can be frozen.) Whip cream to soft peaks and loosely fold through chilled purée.
Serves 4

■ **Port and Prune Fool**
Prepare as for apricot fool using 150g pitted prunes, 125 ml port and zest of ½ lemon in place of apricots, orange juice and sugar. Garnish with sliced almonds.

SYLLABUB CREAM
Whip 300ml chilled cream with 6 tbsp icing sugar to soft peaks then fold in 2 tbsp best sherry or brandy, 4 tbsp lemon juice and the finely grated zest of ½ lemon. Serve chilled. Stored covered in the fridge, it will keep for up to 2 days.
Makes 500 ml

Tangy lemon curd, marbled through whipped cream and punctuated with crumbled meringues, delivers an ethereal pleasure. Acidic fruits such as lemons, limes, passionfruit and berries offset any cloying sweetness. Buy good-quality curd or make your own.

375g caster sugar
220g butter
300 ml lemon juice (about 6 juicy lemons), strained
zest of 1 lemon
6 eggs, lightly beaten with a whisk

lemon curd

PLACE sugar, butter, lemon juice and zest in a pot (use a double boiler if you don't have a thermometer). Heat over medium-low heat until butter has melted. Take off heat and strain eggs into mixture. Return to heat with a thermometer attached and cook, stirring constantly, until temperature reaches 75°C. Or cook in a double boiler until mixture thickens to coat the back of a spoon. REMOVE from heat immediately and stir a little to prevent mixture overheating on base. Bottle while hot in hot, sterilized jars and seal with pop-top seals or store in a sealed container in the fridge.

Makes just over 1 litre
Storage Lemon curd will keep several weeks in the fridge. Bottled preserves will keep as long as the seal remains unbroken.

500 ml chilled cream
1 tsp vanilla extract
185 ml lemon curd, chilled
4 meringues, roughly crushed
garnish 4 tbsp thread coconut, toasted

lemon parfait

WHIP cream with vanilla until it forms soft peaks. Loosely fold in lemon curd and meringues so mixture retains some swirls of the lemon curd.
SPOON into serving bowls and chill until ready to serve. Serve garnished with coconut.

Serves 4-6
Storage Parfaits will keep covered in the fridge for up to 6 hours.

CURD VARIATIONS

Follow the method and use the same ingredients as for lemon curd, changing the flavours to your choice.

LIME CURD

Use 300 ml strained lime juice instead of lemon juice.

PASSIONFRUIT CURD

Use 300 ml strained fresh or frozen passionfruit juice (unsweetened) instead of lemon juice.

flip a crêpe

Make a big batch of crêpes, layer with greaseproof paper and store in the freezer for quick assembly. Or buy ready-made crêpes and keep in the freezer.

1 tbsp butter
2 tbsp sugar
1 tsp vanilla extract
5-6 oranges, peeled and segmented
4 cooked crêpes
4 tbsp whipped cream or crème fraîche
2 tbsp Grand Marnier or Drambuie or brandy

orange flambéed crêpes

HEAT butter, sugar and vanilla in a heavy frypan until melted and sizzling. Add oranges and cook over high heat until mixture comes to a boil, about 1 minute.
HEAT crêpes in microwave for 30 seconds if they have been chilled and place on 4 serving plates.
DIVIDE fruit and sauce between crêpes. Top with cream and fold into 4. Spoon over any pan juices.
HEAT liqueur in microwave for 20 seconds or in a small pot until hot, about 1 minute. Spoon a little hot liqueur over hot crêpes and carefully light. Serve immediately.
Serves 4

250g/2 cups raspberries, fresh or frozen thawed
4 tbsp caster sugar
2 tbsp water

raspberry coulis

PLACE berries in a saucepan with sugar and water. Slowly bring to simmering point over medium heat.
REMOVE from heat and quickly pulse a few times in a food processor to loosely blend. Strain through a sieve to remove seeds. Pour hot coulis into a clean jar. Leave to cool at room temperature.
Makes 500 ml
Storage Store coulis in a sealed container in the fridge. It will keep for a couple of weeks.

CRÊPE BATTER

225 g flour, 350ml milk, 150ml cold water, pinch of salt, 3 eggs, 3 tbsp melted butter
Beat all ingredients except butter together until smooth then beat in butter. The batter should be quite thin.
Lightly grease a pan and cook 1 ladleful at a time, tilting the pan to form a thin, even crêpe. Flip to cook the other side.
Stack the crêpes, cover with plastic wrap and refrigerate.
Makes 12
Storage Crêpes will keep 4-5 days in the fridge if tightly sealed. Freeze with paper or plastic between each crêpe.

BLUEBERRY CRÊPES
Heat blueberry sauce (page 191) and use to fill warmed crêpes.

BANANA RASPBERRY CRÊPES
Fill crêpes with raspberry coulis and slice over bananas.

stir up a crumble

Whether you're after a special dessert for a crowd or a sweet ending to an intimate dinner à deux, you need look no further than crumble. It's sturdy enough to transport to a potluck dinner and smart enough for any company, and it never fails to hit the spot.

250g flour
500g lightly packed brown sugar
180 g fine-cut rolled oats
125 g ground almonds
2 tsp ground cinnamon
½ tsp ground cloves
200g butter, melted

almond and brown sugar crumble topping

COMBINE all ingredients in a bowl. Store in the fridge or freezer until ready to use.

Makes 4¼ cups

500 ml cooked apples or 567g can apples
4 stalks rhubarb cut into 2.5cm pieces
125 g sugar
2 tsp cornflour
½ recipe crumble topping

rhubarb and apple crumble

PREHEAT oven to 180°C. Combine rhubarb, apples, sugar and cornflour. Spread evenly in a large, shallow baking dish, about 30cm in diameter.
SPRINKLE over crumble topping, pressing down with your palm to compact. Bake until topping is crisp and golden, about 50-60 minutes.

Serves 6-8

MAKE IT IN BULK
Crumble topping is useful to make in bulk, as it keeps for ages in the fridge or freezer. Double the recipe for easy use any time.

CHANGE THE FLAVOUR
Use other nuts, eg walnuts, cashews or pecans.Use other spices, eg 1 tsp ground cardamom or allspice for a peach or mango crumble, or for a plain apple crumble add ½ tsp ground cloves.

TRADITIONAL CRUMBLE
For a traditional crumble simply combine equal quantities of brown sugar, butter and flour. Rub the butter into the flour and mix in the sugar. Pile on top of fruit and bake until crispy.

whisk an airy sponge

This recipe doubles or trebles with ease and turns its hand to any incarnation of sponge dessert you fancy, from napoleon cake to butterfly cakes and chocolate rolls. Then again, you may prefer to buy a sponge and start from there. I certainly won't hold it against you.

2 eggs, separated
125g sugar
125g cornflour
1 tbsp flour
1 tsp baking powder

sponge

BEAT egg whites to soft peaks in a clean bowl then beat in sugar until dissolved, about 1 minute. Beat in yolks.
SIFT dry ingredients then add to mixture. Cook as required for recipes that follow.
Storage Cooked sponge will keep in a sealed container for a couple of days and also freezes well.

3 x sponge recipe (above) or
2 readymade 30cm x 25cm
sponges
125 ml raspberry jam
300 ml cream, whipped
icing sugar for dusting

double-layered party sponge

PREHEAT oven to 180°C fanbake. Line 2 sponge roll tins (30cm x 25cm) with baking paper.
PREPARE sponge recipe, spread in tins and bake until risen and sponges bounce back when gently pressed, about 12 minutes. Cool 5 minutes before turning out.
SANDWICH fully cooled sponges with jam and cream. Dust with icing sugar.
Serves 12-16

■ **Double-layered Chocolate Sponge**
Prepare 3 x sponge recipe using 3 tbsp less cornflour and replacing it with 3 tbsp cocoa. Cook as above.

It's easy enough to mix a single recipe of sponge with a hand-held beater or whisk, but if you are doubling or trebling the recipe you will find it much easier with an electric mixer.

raspberry sponge roll

1½ times sponge recipe (page 203), plain or chocolate

8 tbsp raspberry jam or coulis

300ml cream, whipped

PREHEAT oven to 180°C fanbake. Line a 30cm x 25cm sponge roll tin with baking paper.

PREPARE sponge recipe, spread in tin and bake until risen and sponge bounces back when gently pressed, about 12 minutes.

TURN out while hot on to a clean tea towel sprinkled with icing sugar. Remove baking paper and roll up lengthways in the tea towel. Leave to cool.

WHEN ready to serve, carefully unroll, spread with jam and whipped cream then roll up again.

Serves 8-10

napoleon cakes

1½ times sponge recipe cooked as above or use commercial sponge, 24cm x 24cm

1 sheet (160g) puff pastry, cut into 8 rectangles

250 ml cream, whipped to soft peaks

1 punnet strawberries, hulled and thinly sliced

8 tbsp raspberry jam

pink vanilla icing (below)

CUT sponge into 8 pieces.

HEAT oven to 200°C and bake pastries until risen and golden, 15 minutes. Cool and split in half horizontally.

PLACE bottom pieces of pastry on a board and spread with half the cream. Top with strawberries then sponge. Spread sponge with jam and cover with remaining cream and pastry. Ice with pink vanilla icing.

Storage Keep cakes in a cool place and serve within 2 hours or chill up to 8 hours.

To make pink vanilla icing beat together 1½ cups sifted icing sugar, 2 tbsp vanilla extract and ½ drop red food colour.

Serves 8

sponge kisses

1 sponge recipe (previous page)

raspberry jam

icing sugar

PREHEAT oven to 180°C fanbake. Line 12 x 5cm muffin tins with paper patty pans or spray with oil. Divide sponge mixture between prepared tins.

BAKE until risen and mixture bounces back when gently pressed, about 10 minutes. Cool in tins 2 minutes before turning out.

CUT a small round from top of kisses. Spoon a teaspoon of raspberry jam into each hole. Cut sponge top in half and replace on jam like wings. Dust with icing sugar.

Makes 12

To make a terrific fruit sponge dessert, spoon the sponge recipe over fruit and bake. Use cooked sponge (the recipe here or a bought sponge) as the basis for a decadent tiramisu.

500 ml cooked apple
185 ml blueberry sauce (page191)
1 recipe sponge (page 203)

blueberry and apple sponges

PREHEAT oven to 180°C fanbake. Divide apple between 4 x 300-500 ml ramekins. Top with blueberry sauce then sponge mixture.
BAKE until risen and sponge bounces back when gently pressed, about 15-18 minutes.

Serves 4

Variation Use a 400 g can of peaches or apricots instead of apples and blueberry sauce.

4 fresh free-range eggs, separated
4 tbsp brown sugar
250g (1 cup) mascarpone
125 ml strong espresso coffee, cooled
125 ml coffee liqueur or rum
100g piece plain sponge, cut into 2-3cm cubes
garnish 2 tbsp toasted ground hazelnuts or sifted cocoa

tiramisu

BEAT egg yolks and sugar with an electric beater until thick and creamy. Beat in mascarpone and set aside.
In another clean bowl, beat egg whites to soft peaks. Fold gently into mascarpone mixture. Chill while preparing sponge.
COMBINE coffee and liqueur in a bowl. Dunk sponge pieces one at a time into coffee mixture and place in a single layer in 6 small serving bowls to cover base and sides. Spoon mascarpone mixture into each bowl.
SPRINKLE hazelnuts or cocoa over top. Cover and chill for at least 2 hours before serving.

Serves 6

Storage Store in fridge for up to 24 hours.

Variation Prepare as one large dessert in a big bowl, layering sponge and mascarpone.

indulge...
in chocolate

To make great chocolate desserts you need to start with great chocolate. The higher the percentage of cocoa solids the better. Check the packet – anything over 55% and you are on to a good thing. Luxury brands such as Valrhona and Callebaut deliver the goods.

250g dark bittersweet or good-quality eating chocolate, chopped
500 ml chilled cream
4 egg whites
4 tbsp sugar
1 tsp vanilla extract

chocolate mousse

PLACE chocolate and 250 ml of the cream in a saucepan. Stir over gentle heat or microwave at 50% power for
2 minutes until chocolate is melted. Cool.
WHISK egg whites in a clean bowl with sugar until stiff. In another bowl whisk remaining cream with vanilla until it forms firm peaks.
FOLD a third of the egg whites into the cooled chocolate to lighten the mixture. Fold in remaining egg whites then the cream. Chill until quite firm, about 4 hours or up to 24 hours, before serving. Scoop mousse into cups to serve.

Makes 6 cups, serves 8
Storage Prepared mousse can be covered and chilled for up to 48 hours.

155g flour
125g brown sugar
2 tbsp cocoa
2 tsp baking powder
pinch of salt
250 ml milk
3 tbsp melted butter
1 tsp vanilla extract
1 egg
topping 250g brown sugar
2 tbsp cocoa
500 ml boiling water

chocolate fudge pudding

PREHEAT oven to 180°C. Mix dry ingredients together then fold in milk, butter, vanilla and egg, stirring until evenly combined.
DIVIDE mixture between 6 heatproof cups or 300ml ramekins. Sprinkle with combined brown sugar and cocoa. Place cups in a shallow baking tray.
POUR ⅓ cup boiling water over the back of a spoon into each pudding (cups will be full).
BAKE until risen and cooked through, about 20 minutes.

Serves 6

DECADENT CHOCOLATE SAUCE

In a pot or microwave bowl bring 125 ml cream to a simmer (1 minute microwave). Add 250g finely chopped, best quality bitter dark chocolate and mix until smooth. Stir in 2 tbsp liqueur (optional). If you desire a thinner chocolate sauce, add a little more cream.

Makes 375 ml
Storage Sauce will keep in the fridge for up to a week. To soften, reheat in microwave for 1 minute.

tart it up

Cooked sweet pastry shells provide the starting point for a range of great dessert assemblies. Buy shells ready cooked or use frozen pastry. To prepare your own, see page 102.

glazed berry tart with brown sugar mascarpone

250g (1 cup) mascarpone
2 tbsp brown sugar
1 tsp vanilla extract
1 x 23cm cooked and cooled sweet pastry shell
250g fresh berries
4 tbsp raspberry jam
juice of ½ lime

COMBINE mascarpone, brown sugar and vanilla. Spread mixture evenly in pastry shell and cover with berries. Combine jam and lime juice and sieve to remove pips. Drizzle over berries.

Serves 6-8
Variation Prepare as mini tarts to serve as finger food

LEMON CURD TARTS
Buy or make lemon curd (page 196). Spoon into cooked and cooled tart cases – individual tarts will use about 2 tbsp; allow 250 ml for a 23cm tart. Garnish with toasted thread coconut or fresh berries.

CHOCOLATE TARTS
Spoon decadent chocolate sauce (page 208) into cooked and cooled tart cases. Chill or freeze. Garnish with cherries or berries.

CREAM CHEESE AND BERRY TARTS
Soften 250g cream cheese and mix in the zest of ½ lemon and 2 tbsp icing sugar. Spread in cooked and cooled tart cases and top with sliced berries.

bake with fruity fillings

2 x 24cm sheets puff pastry or 320g, rolled thinly
90g (¾ cup) ground almonds
4 tbsp sugar
1 tsp vanilla extract
½ tsp almond essence
1 egg white
4 just-ripe pears, halved and cored
glaze 2 tbsp apricot jam
1 tbsp water

free-form pear and almond tarts

PREHEAT oven to 200°C. Cut pastry into 8 x 10cm rounds. Place on a baking tray, allowing a little space between each round.

COMBINE almonds, sugar, vanilla, almond essence and egg white. Divide evenly between pastry rounds, about 1 tbsp per tart, leaving the pastry rim clean.

THINLY slice pears and arrange on top of each tart. Bake until pastry starts to puff, about 10 minutes, then reduce temperature to 160°C and cook until tarts are golden, fruit is tender and pastry cooked through, about 15-20 minutes.

MELT apricot jam in microwave for 30 seconds, thin with water and pass through a sieve. Brush over hot tarts.

Makes 8

■ **Apple and Almond Tarts**
Use 4 tart apples in place of the pears.
■ **Apricot and Almond Tarts**
Use 4 large fresh apricots in place of the pears.

2 x 24cm sheets puff pastry or 320g, rolled thinly
2 large tasty apples, peeled, quartered and cored
250 ml hot water
125 ml golden syrup

caramel apple turnovers

PREHEAT oven to 200°C. Cut pastry into 8 squares and place an apple quarter in the centre of each one. Draw up pastry to enclose apple, pinching edges to seal.

PLACE in a baking dish, allowing a little room between each. Mix water and golden syrup and pour over pies.

BAKE until golden and cooked through, about 20 minutes. Serve with syrup spooned over.

Makes 8, serve 1-2 per person

■ **Caramel Pear Turnovers**
Use 2 pears, peeled, cored and quartered, in place of the apples.
■ **Caramel Mango Turnovers**
Use 2 mangoes, peeled and diced, in place of apples.

treat yourself

Buttery, melt-in-the-mouth Russian fudge, creamy coconut ice and chunky fudge cake made with cookies are heaven on a plate for the sweet toothed amongst us and good for take-a-plate treats.

microwave russian fudge

750g sugar
125 ml milk
½ can (200g) sweetened condensed milk
1 tsp golden syrup
100 g butter
pinch of salt
1 tsp vanilla extract
optional 125 g chopped walnuts

COMBINE all ingredients except nuts in a very large microwave-proof jug. Cover and microwave on high for 10-12 minutes, stirring well every 2 minutes. Fudge should be a rich golden colour.

BEAT until thick with a wooden spoon or electric beater, about 4 minutes. Add walnuts if using and pour into a greased or lined 16cm x 18cm tin. Cut into small pieces when set.

To cook fudge on the stove top, bring ingredients to the boil in a large pot and stir constantly over heat until mixture reaches soft ball stage (see glossary), about 15 minutes. Pour into prepared tin and leave to set.

Makes about 24 pieces

Storage Fudge will keep for several weeks in a sealed container.

chocolate icing

450g icing sugar
2 tbsp cocoa
50g butter, melted
3 tbsp boiling water
1 tsp vanilla extract

BEAT together until smooth and creamy.

coconut ice

150g butter
375g icing sugar
225g desiccated coconut
4 tbsp milk
1 tsp vanilla extract
1 tsp lemon juice
few drops red food colour

MELT butter in a pot. Mix in icing sugar, coconut, milk, vanilla, lemon juice and food colour and beat hard with a wooden spoon until evenly combined.

SPREAD in a lined tin about 16cm x 16cm and chill until set, about 2 hours, before cutting.

Makes about 24 pieces

Storage Coconut ice will keep for up to 2 weeks in an airtight container in a cool place.

favourite chocolate fudge cake

2 eggs, lightly beaten
240g butter
185g sugar
3 tbsp cocoa
1 tsp vanilla extract
2 packets wine biscuits (500g), crushed
garnish 1 recipe chocolate icing (see left)

PLACE eggs, butter, sugar, cocoa and vanilla in a pot over low heat. Stir constantly, removing mixture from heat just before it comes to a simmer. Mix in biscuits.

PRESS mixture firmly into a 30cm x 25cm sponge roll tin. Ice with chocolate icing. Cut into pieces when set.

Makes 32 pieces

Storage This will keep for 2 weeks in an airtight container in a cool place.

crumb sweet biscuits

100g butter
185 ml sweetened condensed milk
250g plain sweet biscuits, crushed to fine crumbs
150g dried apricots, finely chopped
90g desiccated coconut
2 tbsp lemon juice
icing 450g icing sugar
50g butter, melted
3 tbsp boiling water
1 tbsp lemon juice

apricot coconut slice

MELT butter with condensed milk, bring to the boil and simmer over very low heat for 2 minutes, stirring several times. Remove from heat.

ADD biscuit crumbs, apricots, coconut and lemon juice and mix well.

PRESS into a 30cm x 24cm baking tin or sponge roll tin lined with baking paper. Chill until set.

MIX icing ingredients together until smooth. Spread over base. Cut into pieces.

Makes about 24 slices

Storage This will keep for 2 weeks in an airtight container in a cool place.

350g good-quality dark eating chocolate, chopped
185 ml caramel condensed milk
2 tsp vanilla extract
8 crumbled plain sweet biscuits
200g roughly chopped dried apricots
75g chopped brazil nuts or almonds
2 tbsp icing sugar
garnish melted chocolate

fruit and nut caramel chocolate balls

PLACE chocolate and condensed milk in a large microwave-proof bowl. Microwave on high for about 2 minutes, stirring every 30 seconds, until melted and smooth.

MIX in vanilla, biscuits, apricots, nuts and icing sugar. Mixture will be very thick.

ROLL mixture into balls and flatten slightly before drizzling with melted chocolate. Alternatively, press mixture firmly into a 24cm x16cm shallow tin lined with plastic wrap and drizzle with chocolate. Chill until set then cut into slices.

Makes about 30 balls

Storage These keep for 2 weeks in the fridge.

in the kitchen

Knowing how your oven cooks, using the same set of measures throughout a recipe and being familiar with cooking terms ensures your success in the kitchen.

oven heat

Recipes in this book were tested in a fan-forced oven so if you use a non-fan oven you may need to add about 10% to the cooking time or increase the heat by 5-10°C. Brand to brand and kitchen to kitchen, ovens cook differently. For this reason, and also because ingredients differ in their moisture content and ability to absorb liquid etc, you do need to use your judgement and treat the cooking times in recipes as a guide. Until you get used to your oven check 10-15% before the specified time to see how things are proceeding. As you cook more you will see where your oven sits in relation to this book and will be able to judge how to amend the times accordingly. Remember, too, to preheat the oven to the specified temperature before you start cooking.

measures used in this book

1 cup equals 250ml (8 fl oz)
1 tbsp (tablespoon) equals 15ml
1 tsp (teaspoon) equals 5ml
A ruler can be found on the inside back flap.

saving on washing up

No one likes to be faced with a mountain of dishes. Wash up and tidy as you go while cooking – it's really hard to cook or think in a mess. Baking paper is incredibly useful as a liner for oven baking to stop sticking and save on washing up. I use it wherever I can to line pans before pie making, grilling or roasting – unless I want the caramelization created by juices in a roasting pan for some gravy. Soak the mashed potato pot as soon as you've dished up – this stuff could stand in for glue. Should you be unlucky enough to burn a pot, fill it with water, add 1 tsp dishwasher powder and boil for 5 minutes. Most burnt pots can be remedied in this way.

cooking terms

Blanch drop vegetables quickly into boiling water, then cool in cold water. This sets a fresh colour.

Blitz pulse or blend in a food processor.

Coring tomatoes use a small, sharp knife to cut out the stem cores from tomatoes; they are always tough and unpalatable.

Dice chop into small pieces, about 1cm.

Finely dice chop into smaller pieces, about ½ cm.

Fold very gently combine mixtures with a large scooping motion using a large, flat spoon.

Hull remove the cores from berries.

Non-corrosive bowl acidic ingredients should never be put into aluminium or other corrosive metal bowls. Use a plastic or glass container.

Purée blend until smooth.

Season add salt and pepper to taste. Sea salt is usually coarser than fine salt and weighs less per spoonful.

Soft ball stage the stage when boiling sugar syrup at which it will form a soft ball when a small amount is dropped into a glass of very cold water. Roll it between your fingers – the mixture should hold its shape but be soft and pliable. On a candy thermometer the temperature is 115°C.

Soft peaks whipping cream or egg whites to a point where when you lift the beater the mixture forms peaks that are soft at the top and may curl. At firm peak stage the peaks stand up firmly.

Toasting nuts either place nuts on a baking tray and bake at 180°C until they smell aromatic and are golden, about 12-15 minutes, or microwave ½ cup at a time for 2-3 minutes, stirring every 30 seconds.

Zest the thin, aromatic, oily outer skin of citrus fruits. Take care not to include the white pith underneath, which is bitter.

Lemon pasta with peas and prawns (page 53)

index

223

thank you…

I never cease to be amazed by the sheer slog that goes into making a cookbook. From the initial design to the pages that you see in front of you, the efforts, energies and talents of a number of people come to bear, and to them I would like to extend my heartfelt thanks.

Firstly to Nick Tresidder for such gorgeous images, thank you. It's been a great pleasure to work with you again. Many thanks to designer Karryn Muschamp for the smooth, seamless design of this book. To Natalie Keys, thanks once again for working tirelessly behind the scenes to put the book together on the page and manage the production process. Sally Butters, a big thank you for your thoughtful editing, and Jane Turner for all your careful checking. In the test kitchen Angela Casley and Glenys Cennamo, thanks for your trusty palates and help in road-mapping the recipes for easy use. Sarah Lods, thanks for finding great props and helping to make the images look so good.

In my office thanks go to Lesley MacMichael and Joy Danford. To my lovely family and friends, thanks for your support, for putting up with my lengthy disappearance into the production tunnel and for being such good guinea pigs. Special thanks to Margot Baddeley and Kirsten Tweedie.

Many of the props used in this book have been kindly loaned.
Thank you to Nest, Living & Giving, The Epicurean Workshop, Milly's, Corso de' Fiori and Bodum. And Michelle Donaldson for the lovely necklaces.

And finally, thanks to my good cooking mates out there who have shared ideas and delicious recipes and to the chefs, cooks and food writers around the world who have inspired and nourished my interest in food.

Annabel 2006